Warning-Disclaimer

The purpose of this book is to educate and entertain. The author or publisher does not guarantee that anyone following the techniques, suggestions, tips, ideas, or strategies will become successful. The author and publisher shall have neither liability or responsibility to anyone with respect to any loss or damage caused, or alleged to be caused, directly or indirectly by the information contained in this book.

CONTENTS

DIABETES DIET

A diabetes diet simply means eating the healthiest foods in moderate amounts and sticking to regular mealtimes.

A diabetes diet is a healthy-eating plan that's naturally rich in nutrients and low in fat and calories. Key elements are fruits, vegetables and whole grains. In fact, a diabetes diet is the best eating plan for most everyone.

Why do you need to develop a healthy-eating plan?

If you have diabetes or prediabetes, your doctor will likely recommend that you see a dietitian to help you develop a healthy-eating plan. The plan helps you control your blood sugar (glucose), manage your weight and control heart disease risk factors, such as high blood pressure and high blood fats.

When you eat extra calories and fat, your body creates an undesirable rise in blood glucose. If blood glucose isn't kept in check, it can lead to serious problems, such as a high blood glucose level (hyperglycemia) that, if persistent, may lead to long-term complications, such as nerve, kidney and heart damage.

You can help keep your blood glucose level in a safe range by making healthy food choices and tracking your eating habits.

For most people with type 2 diabetes, weight loss also can make it easier to control blood glucose and offers a host of other health benefits. If you need to lose weight, a diabetes diet provides a well-organized, nutritious way to reach your goal safely.

Recommended foods

Make your calories count with these nutritious foods. Choose healthy carbohydrates, fiber-rich foods, fish and "good" fats.

Healthy carbohydrates

During digestion, sugars (simple carbohydrates) and starches (complex carbohydrates) break down into blood glucose. Focus on healthy carbohydrates, such as:

- Fruits
- Vegetables

- Whole grains
- Legumes, such as beans and peas
- Low-fat dairy products, such as milk and cheese

Avoid less healthy carbohydrates, such as foods or drinks with added fats, sugars and sodium.

Fiber-rich foods

Dietary fiber includes all parts of plant foods that your body can't digest or absorb. Fiber moderates how your body digests and helps control blood sugar levels. Foods high in fiber include:

- Vegetables
- Fruits
- Nuts
- Legumes, such as beans and peas
- Whole grains

Heart-healthy fish

Eat heart-healthy fish at least twice a week. Fish such as salmon, mackerel, tuna and sardines are rich in omega-3 fatty acids, which may prevent heart disease.

Avoid fried fish and fish with high levels of mercury, such as king mackerel.

'Good' fats

Foods containing monounsaturated and polyunsaturated fats can help lower your cholesterol levels. These include:

- Avocados
- Nuts
- Canola, olive and peanut oils

But don't overdo it, as all fats are high in calories.

Foods to avoid

Diabetes increases your risk of heart disease and stroke by accelerating the development of clogged and hardened arteries. Foods containing the following can work against your goal of a heart-healthy diet.

- **Saturated fats.** Avoid high-fat dairy products and animal proteins such as butter, beef, hot dogs, sausage and bacon. Also limit coconut and palm kernel oils.

- **Trans fats.** Avoid trans fats found in processed snacks, baked goods, shortening and stick margarines.
- **Cholesterol.** Cholesterol sources include high-fat dairy products and high-fat animal proteins, egg yolks, liver, and other organ meats. Aim for no more than 200 milligrams (mg) of cholesterol a day.
- **Sodium.** Aim for less than 2,300 mg of sodium a day. Your doctor may suggest you aim for even less if you have high blood pressure.

What are the results of a diabetes diet?

Embracing your healthy-eating plan is the best way to keep your blood glucose level under control and prevent diabetes complications. And if you need to lose weight, you can tailor it to your specific goals.

Aside from managing your diabetes, a diabetes diet offers other benefits, too. Because a diabetes diet recommends generous amounts of fruits, vegetables and fiber, following it is likely to reduce your risk of cardiovascular diseases and certain types of cancer. And consuming low-fat dairy products can reduce your risk of low bone mass in the future.

Are there any risks?

If you have diabetes, it's important that you partner with your doctor and dietitian to create an eating plan that works for you. Use healthy foods, portion control and scheduling to manage your blood glucose level. If you stray from your prescribed diet, you run the risk of fluctuating blood sugar levels and more-serious complications.

14-Day Meal Plan

Meal Plan	Breakfast	Lunch	Dinner
Day-1	Cheesy Spinach And Egg Casserole	Baked Salmon Cakes	Crispy Baked Tofu
Day-2	Zucchini Bread	Unstuffed Cabbage	Turkey & Brown Rice Lettuce Cups
Day-3	Cranberry Coffeecake	Tilapia With Coconut Rice	Asian Cold Noodle Salad
Day-4	Scrumptious Orange Muffins	Italian Pork Chops	Beef Fajitas
Day-5	Scotch Eggs	Air Fried Zucchini Blooms	Stir-fried Steak And Cabbage
Day-6	Easy Turkey Breakfast Patties	Turkey Cobb Salad	Chicken Tuscany
Day-7	Fried Egg	Shrimp And Black Bean Salad	Italian Steamed Mussels
Day-8	Blueberry Buns	Quick And Easy Shrimp Stir-fry	Tuna Carbonara
Day-9	Pumpkin Muffins	Pork Loin With Onion Beer Sauce	Grilled Vegetable & Noodle Salad
Day-10	Savory Breakfast Egg Bites	Shrimp & Avocado Salad	Garden Vegetable Pasta
Day-11	Pumpkin Pie Smoothie	Pan Seared Trout & Salsa	Popcorn Style Cauliflower
Day-12	Soft Pretzel Bites	Scallops And Asparagus Skillet	Holiday Apple & Cranberry Salad
Day-13	Homemade Turkey Breakfast Sausage	Grilled Tuna Steaks	Cabbage Slaw Salad
Day-14	Falafel With Creamy Garlic-yogurt Sauce	Broiled Teriyaki Salmon	Tex Mex Veggie Bake

BREAKFAST RECIPES

Cheesy Spinach And Egg Casserole

Servings:8
Cooking Time: 35 Minutes

Ingredients:

- 1 (10-ounce / 284-g) package frozen spinach, thawed and drained
- 1 (14-ounce / 397-g) can artichoke hearts, drained
- ¼ cup finely chopped red bell pepper
- 8 eggs, lightly beaten
- ¼ cup unsweetened plain almond milk
- 2 garlic cloves, minced
- ½ teaspoon salt
- ½ teaspoon freshly ground black pepper
- ½ cup crumbled goat cheese
- Nonstick cooking spray

Directions:

1. Preheat the oven to 375ºF (190ºC). Spray a baking dish with nonstick cooking spray and set aside.
2. Mix the spinach, artichoke hearts, bell peppers, beaten eggs, almond milk, garlic, salt, and pepper in a large bowl, and stir to incorporate.
3. Pour the mixture into the greased baking dish and scatter the goat cheese on top.
4. Bake in the preheated oven for 35 minutes, or until the top is lightly golden around the edges and eggs are set.
5. Remove from the oven and serve warm.

Nutrition:

- Infocalories: 105 | fat: 4.8g | protein: 8.9g | carbs: 6.1g | fiber: 1.7g | sugar: 1.0g| sodium: 486mg

Zucchini Bread

Servings: 8
Cooking Time: 40 Minutes

Ingredients:
- ¾ cup shredded zucchini
- 1/2 cup almond flour
- 1/4 teaspoon salt
- 1/4 cup cocoa powder, unsweetened
- 1/2 cup chocolate chips, unsweetened, divided
- 6 tablespoons erythritol sweetener
- 1/2 teaspoon baking soda
- 2 tablespoons olive oil
- 1/2 teaspoon vanilla extract, unsweetened
- 2 tablespoons butter, unsalted, melted
- 1 egg, pastured

Directions:
1. Switch on the air fryer, insert fryer basket, grease it with olive oil, then shut with its lid, set the fryer at 310 degrees F and preheat for 10 minutes.
2. Meanwhile, place flour in a bowl, add salt, cocoa powder and baking soda and stir until mixed.
3. Crack the eggs in another bowl, whisk in sweetener, egg, oil, butter, and vanilla until smooth and then slowly whisk in flour mixture until incorporated.
4. Add zucchini along with 1/3 cup chocolate chips and then fold until just mixed.
5. Take a mini loaf pan that fits into the air fryer, grease it with olive oil, then pour in the prepared batter and sprinkle remaining chocolate chips on top.
6. Open the fryer, place the loaf pan in it, close with its lid and cook for 30 minutes at the 310 degrees F until inserted toothpick into the bread slides out clean.
7. When air fryer beeps, open its lid, remove the loaf pan, then place it on a wire rack and let the bread cool in it for 20 minutes.
8. Take out the bread, let it cool completely, then cut it into slices and serve.

Nutrition:
- InfoCalories: 356 Cal Carbs: 2 g Fat: 10 g Protein: 8 g Fiber: 2.5 g

Cranberry Coffeecake

Servings: 12

Cooking Time: 20-25 Minutes

Ingredients:

- 1 cup whole fresh cranberries
- 4 large eggs
- What you'll need from store cupboard:
- 1 ¼ cup flax seed meal
- ½ cup Splenda
- ½ cup sugar free vanilla syrup
- ¼ cup olive oil
- 3 tbsp. cinnamon
- 1 tbsp. vanilla
- 1 tsp baking powder
- 1 tsp nutmeg
- ½ tsp salt
- Nonstick cooking spray

Directions:

1. Heat oven to 350 degrees. Coat a Bundt cake pan with cooking spray.
2. Put cranberries in a microwave safe bowl and cover with plastic wrap. Cook on high 1-2 minutes or the berries are tender.
3. In a medium mixing bowl combine all the wet Ingredients. Mix until thoroughly combined.
4. Add the dry Ingredients and mix well. Let sit for 10 minutes so the mixture thickens.
5. Fold in the cranberries and pour into prepared pan.
6. Bake 20-25 minutes or until the coffeecake passes the toothpick test. Let cook 5 minutes in pan then invert onto serving plate.

Nutrition:

- InfoCalories 122 Total Carbs 11g Net Carbs 9g Protein 2g Fat 6g Sugar 9g Fiber 2g

Scrumptious Orange Muffins

Servings:8
Cooking Time: 15 Minutes

Ingredients:

- Dry Ingredients:
- 2½ cups finely ground almond flour
- ½ teaspoon baking powder
- ½ teaspoon ground cardamom
- ¾ teaspoon ground cinnamon
- ¼ teaspoon salt

- Wet Ingredients:
- 2 large eggs
- 4 tablespoons avocado or coconut oil
- 1 tablespoon raw honey
- ¼ teaspoon vanilla extract
- Grated zest and juice of 1 medium orange
- Special Equipment:
- An 8-cup muffin tin

Directions:

1. Preheat the oven to 375ºF (190ºC) and line an 8-cup muffin tin with paper liners.
2. Stir together the almond flour, baking powder, cardamon, cinnamon, and salt in a large bowl. Set aside.
3. Whisk together the eggs, oil, honey, vanilla, zest and juice in a medium bowl. Pour the mixture into the bowl of dry ingredients and stir with a spatula just until incorporated.
4. Pour the batter into the prepared muffin cups, filling each about three-quarters full.
5. Bake in the preheated oven for 15 minutes, or until the tops are golden and a toothpick inserted in the center comes out clean.
6. Let the muffins cool for 10 minutes before serving.

Nutrition:

- Infocalories: 287 | fat: 23.5g | protein: 7.9g | carbs: 15.8g | fiber: 3.8g | sugar: 9.8g| sodium: 96mg

Scotch Eggs

Servings: 4
Cooking Time: 15 Minutes

Ingredients:
- 1-pound pork sausage, pastured
- 2 tablespoons chopped parsley
- 1/8 teaspoon salt
- 1/8 teaspoon grated nutmeg
- 1 tablespoon chopped chives
- 1/8 teaspoon ground black pepper
- 2 teaspoons ground mustard and more as needed
- 4 eggs, hard-boiled, shell peeled
- 1 cup shredded parmesan cheese, low-fat

Directions:
1. Switch on the air fryer, insert fryer basket, grease it with olive oil, then shut with its lid, set the fryer at 400 degrees F and preheat for 10 minutes.
2. Meanwhile, place sausage in a bowl, add salt, black pepper, parsley, chives, nutmeg, and mustard, then stir until well mixed and shape the mixture into four patties.
3. Peel each boiled egg, then place an egg on a patty and shape the meat around it until the egg has evenly covered.
4. Place cheese in a shallow dish, and then roll the egg in the cheese until covered completely with cheese; prepare remaining eggs in the same manner.
5. Then open the fryer, add eggs in it close with its lid and cook for 15 minutes at the 400 degrees F until nicely golden and crispy, turning the eggs and spraying with oil halfway through the frying.
6. When air fryer beeps, open its lid, transfer eggs onto a serving plate and serve with mustard.

Nutrition:
- Info Calories: 533 Cal Carbs: 0.6 g Fat: 7 g Protein: 6.3 g Fiber: 0 g

Easy Turkey Breakfast Patties

Servings:8
Cooking Time: 10 Minutes

Ingredients:

- 1 pound (454 g) lean ground turkey
- ½ teaspoon dried thyme
- ½ teaspoon dried sage
- ½ teaspoon salt
- ½ teaspoon freshly ground black pepper
- ¼ teaspoon ground fennel seeds
- 1 teaspoon extra-virgin olive oil

Directions:

1. Mix the ground turkey, thyme, sage, salt, pepper, and fennel in a large bowl, and stir until well combined.
2. Form the turkey mixture into 8 equal-sized patties with your hands.
3. In a skillet, heat the olive oil over medium-high heat. Cook the patties for 3 to 4 minutes per side until cooked through.
4. Transfer the patties to a plate and serve hot.

Nutrition:

- Info(1 Patty)calories: 91 | fat: 4.8g | protein: 11.2g | carbs: 0.1g | fiber: 0.1g | sugar: 0g| sodium: 155mg

Fried Egg

Servings: 1
Cooking Time: 4 Minutes

Ingredients:
- 1 egg, pastured
- 1/8 teaspoon salt
- 1/8 teaspoon cracked black pepper

Directions:
1. Take the fryer pan, grease it with olive oil and then crack the egg in it.
2. Switch on the air fryer, insert fryer pan, then shut with its lid, and set the fryer at 370 degrees F.
3. Set the frying time to 3 minutes, then when the air fryer beep, open its lid and check the egg; if egg needs more cooking, then air fryer it for another minute.
4. Transfer the egg to a serving plate, season with salt and black pepper and serve.

Nutrition:
- Info Calories: 90 Cal Carbs: 0.6 g Fat: 7 g Protein: 6.3 g Fiber: 0 g

Blueberry Buns

Servings: 6
Cooking Time: 12 Minutes

Ingredients:
- 240g all-purpose flour
- 50g granulated sugar
- 8g baking powder
- 2g of salt
- 85g chopped cold butter
- 85g of fresh blueberries
- 3g grated fresh ginger
- 113 ml whipping cream
- 2 large eggs
- 4 ml vanilla extract
- 5 ml of water

Directions:
1. Put sugar, flour, baking powder and salt in a large bowl.
2. Put the butter with the flour using a blender or your hands until the mixture resembles thick crumbs.
3. Mix the blueberries and ginger in the flour mixture and set aside
4. Mix the whipping cream, 1 egg and the vanilla extract in a different container.
5. Put the cream mixture with the flour mixture until combined.
6. Shape the dough until it reaches a thickness of approximately 38 mm and cut it into eighths.
7. Spread the buns with a combination of egg and water. Set aside Preheat the air fryer set it to 180°C.
8. Place baking paper in the preheated inner basket and place the buns on top of the paper. Cook for 12 minutes at 180°C, until golden brown

Nutrition:
- InfoCalories: 105 Fat: 1.64g Carbohydrates: 20.09gProtein: 2.43g Sugar: 2.1g Cholesterol: 0mg

Pumpkin Muffins

Servings: 10
Cooking Time: 20 Minutes

Ingredients:

- 2 eggs
- ¼ cup butter, melted
- What you'll need from store cupboard:
- 2 cup almond flour
- ¾ cup pumpkin
- ⅓ cup Splenda
- 2 tbsp. pumpkin seeds
- 2 tsp baking powder
- 1 tsp cinnamon
- 1 tsp vanilla
- ½ tsp salt

Directions:

1. Heat oven to 400 degrees. Line a muffin pan with paper liners.
2. In a large bowl, combine butter, pumpkin, eggs and vanilla. Whisk until smooth.
3. In another bowl, combine flour, Splenda, baking powder, cinnamon and salt. Add to pumpkin mixture and stir to combine. Divide evenly between muffin cups.
4. Sprinkle the pumpkin seeds on the top and bake 20 minutes, or they pass the toothpick test.
5. Let cool 10 minutes before serving.

Nutrition:

- InfoCalories 212 Total Carbs 13g Net Carbs 10g Protein 6g Fat 16g Sugar 8g Fiber 3g

Savory Breakfast Egg Bites

Servings:8
Cooking Time: 20 To 25 Minutes

Ingredients:
- 6 eggs, beaten
- ¼ cup unsweetened plain almond milk
- ¼ cup crumbled goat cheese
- ½ cup sliced brown mushrooms
- 1 cup chopped spinach
- ¼ cup sliced sun-dried tomatoes
- 1 red bell pepper, diced
- Salt and freshly ground black pepper, to taste
- Nonstick cooking spray
- Special Equipment:
- An 8-cup muffin tin

Directions:
1. Preheat the oven to 350ºF (180ºC). Grease an 8-cup muffin tin with nonstick cooking spray.
2. Make the egg bites: Mix together the beaten eggs, almond milk, cheese, mushroom, spinach, tomatoes, bell pepper, salt, and pepper in a large bowl, and whisk to combine.
3. Spoon the mixture into the prepared muffin cups, filling each about three-quarters full.
4. Bake in the preheated oven for 20 to 25 minutes, or until the top is golden brown and a fork comes out clean.
5. Let the egg bites sit for 5 minutes until slightly cooled. Remove from the muffin tin and serve warm.

Nutrition:
- Info(1 Egg Bite)calories: 68 | fat: 4.1g | protein: 6.2g | carbs: 2.9g | fiber: 1.1g | sugar: 2.0g| sodium: 126mg

Ham & Jicama Hash

Servings: 4
Cooking Time: 15 Minutes

Ingredients:
- 6 eggs, beaten
- 2 cups jicama, grated
- 1 cup low fat cheddar cheese, grated
- 1 cup ham, diced
- What you'll need from store cupboard:
- Salt and pepper, to taste
- Nonstick cooking spray

Directions:
1. Spray a large nonstick skillet with cooking spray and place over medium-high heat. Add jicama and cook, stirring occasionally, until it starts to brown, about 5 minutes.
2. Add remaining Ingredients and reduce heat to medium. Cook about 3 minutes, then flip over and cook until eggs are set, about 3-5 minutes more. Season with salt and pepper and serve.

Nutrition:
- InfoCalories 221 Total Carbs 8g Net Carbs 5g Protein 21g Fat 11g Sugar 2g Fiber 3g

Mocha Java Smoothies

Servings: 4
Cooking Time: 3 Minutes

Ingredients:

- 3 cup skim milk
- ¼ cup egg substitute, cholesterol free
- What you'll need from store cupboard:
- 3 tbsp. Splenda
- 3 tbsp. unsweetened cocoa
- 2 tsp instant coffee granules
- 1 ½ tsp vanilla

Directions:

1. Place all Ingredients in a blender and process until smooth. Pour into glasses and serve immediately.

Nutrition:

- InfoCalories 151 Total Carbs 21g Net Carbs 20g Protein 12g Fat 1g Sugar 19g Fiber 1g

Pumpkin Pie Smoothie

Servings:2
Cooking Time: 5 Minutes

Ingredients:
- 1 ½ cup almond milk, unsweetened
- 4 oz. reduced fat cream cheese, soft
- ½ cup Greek yogurt
- What you'll need from store cupboard:
- ¼ cup pumpkin puree
- 2 tbsp. Splenda
- 1/8 tsp cinnamon
- Pinch ginger

Directions:
1. Place all Ingredients in a blender. Process until smooth and everything is combined.
2. Pour into two glasses and garnish with the pinch of ginger on top.

Nutrition:
- InfoCalories 220 Total Carbs 27g Net Carbs 25g Protein 13g Fat 5g Sugar 15g Fiber 2g

LUNCH AND DINNER RECIPES

Baked Salmon Cakes

Servings: 4
Cooking Time: 20 Minutes

Ingredients:

- 15 ounces canned salmon, drained
- 1 large egg, whisked
- 2 teaspoons Dijon mustard
- 1 small yellow onion, minced
- 1 ½ cups whole-wheat breadcrumbs
- ¼ cup low-fat mayonnaise
- ¼ cup nonfat Greek yogurt, plain
- 1 tablespoon fresh chopped parsley
- 1 tablespoon fresh lemon juice
- 2 green onions, sliced thin

Directions:

1. Preheat the oven to 450°F and line a baking sheet with parchment.
2. Flake the salmon into a medium bowl then stir in the egg and mustard.
3. Mix in the onions and breadcrumbs by hand, blending well, then shape into 8 patties.
4. Grease a large skillet and heat it over medium heat.
5. Add the patties and fry for 2 minutes on each side until browned.
6. Transfer the patties to the baking sheet and bake for 15 minutes or until cooked through.
7. Meanwhile, whisk together the remaining ingredients.

Nutrition:

- Info Calories 240, Total Fat 12.2g, Saturated Fat 1.4g, Total Carbs 9.3g, Net Carbs 7.8g, Protein 25g, Sugar 1.8g, Fiber 1.5g, Sodium 241mg

Unstuffed Cabbage

Servings: X

Cooking Time: 20 Minutes

Ingredients:

- 1-tablespoon olive oil
- 1 small onion, chopped
- 1½ cups chopped green cabbage
- 16 precooked frozen meatballs
- 1 cup frozen cooked rice
- 2 tomatoes, chopped
- ½ teaspoon dried marjoram
- Pinch salt
- Freshly ground black pepper

Directions:

1. In a 6-inch metal bowl, combine the oil and the onion. Bake for 2 to 4 minutes or until the onion is crisp and tender.
2. Add the cabbage, meatballs, rice, tomatoes, marjoram, salt, and pepper, and stir.
3. Bake for 12 to 16 minutes, stirring once during cooking time, until the meatballs are hot, the rice is warmed, and the vegetables are tender.

Nutrition:

- Info Calories: 453; Total Fat: 20g; Saturated Fat: 7g; Cholesterol: 47mg; Sodium: 590mg;Carbohydrates: 51g; Fiber: 4g; Protein: 25g

Tilapia With Coconut Rice

Servings: 4
Cooking Time: 15 Minutes

Ingredients:

- 4 (6-ounce) boneless tilapia fillets
- 1 tablespoon ground turmeric
- Salt and pepper
- 1 tablespoon olive oil
- 2 (8.8-ounce) packets precooked whole-grain rice
- 1 cup light coconut milk, shaken
- ½ cup fresh chopped cilantro
- 1 ½ tablespoons fresh lime juice

Directions:

1. Season the fish with turmeric, salt, and pepper.
2. Heat the oil in a large skillet over medium heat and add the fish.
3. Cook for 2 to 3 minutes per side until golden brown.
4. Remove the fish to a plate and cover to keep warm.
5. Reheat the skillet and add the rice, coconut milk, and a pinch of salt.
6. Simmer on high heat until thickened, about 3 to 4 minutes.
7. Stir in the cilantro and lime juice.
8. Spoon the rice onto plates and serve with the cooked fish.

Nutrition:

- Info Calories 460, Total Fat 25.2g, Saturated Fat 15.3g, Total Carbs 27.1g, Net Carbs 23.4g, Protein 34.8g, Sugar 2.4g, Fiber 3.7g, Sodium 145mg

Air Fried Zucchini Blooms

Servings: 3
Cooking Time: 3-5 Minutes

Ingredients:
- 2½ pounds zucchini flowers, rinsed
- 1 cup almond flour, finely milled
- Pinch of sea salt, to taste
- Balsamic vinegar, for garnish

Directions:
1. Preheat Air Fryer to 330 degrees F.
2. Half-fill deep fryer with oil. Set this at medium heat. Lightly season zucchini flowers with salt, and then dredge in almond flour.
3. Layer breaded flowers into the Air Fryer basket Fry until golden brown. Drain on paper towels. Transfer to a plate. Pour balsamic vinegar if using. Serve.

Nutrition:
- Info Calorie: 117Carbohydrate: 8g Fat: 8g Protein: 1g Fiber: 0g

Italian Pork Chops

Servings: 4
Cooking Time: 45 Minutes

Ingredients:
- 4 pork chops, boneless
- 3 garlic cloves, minced
- 1 tsp. dried rosemary, crushed
- ¼ tsp. pepper
- ¼ tsp. sea salt

Directions:
1. Preheat the oven to 425 F/ 218 C.
2. Line baking tray with cooking spray and season pork chops with pepper and salt.
3. Combine garlic and rosemary and rub all over pork chops.
4. Place pork chops in a prepared baking tray.
5. Roast pork chops in preheated oven for 10 minutes.
6. Turn oven temperature to 350 F/ 180 C and roast for 25 minutes.

Nutrition:
- Info Calories 261Fat 19.9 g, Carbohydrates 1 g,Sugar 0 g,Protein 18.1 g,Cholesterol 69 mg

Shrimp And Black Bean Salad

Servings: 6
Cooking Time: None

Ingredients:
- ¼ cup apple cider vinegar
- 3 tablespoons olive oil
- 1 teaspoon ground cumin
- ½ teaspoon chipotle chili powder
- ¼ teaspoon salt
- 1 pound cooked shrimp, peeled and deveined
- 1 (15-ounce) can black beans, rinsed and drained
- 1 cup diced tomatoes
- 1 small green pepper, diced
- ¼ cup sliced green onions
- ¼ cup fresh chopped cilantro

Directions:
1. Whisk together the vinegar, olive oil, cumin, chili powder, and salt in a large bowl.
2. Chop the shrimp into bite-sized pieces then add to the bowl.
3. Toss in the beans, tomatoes, bell pepper, green onion, and cilantro until well combined.
4. Cover until ready to serve.

Nutrition:
- Info Calories 375, Total Fat 15gSaturated Fat 3.1g, Total Carbs 36.3g, Net Carbs 28.2g,Protein 26.2g, Sugar 8.3g, Fiber 8.1g, Sodium 627mg

Turkey Cobb Salad

Servings: 4
Cooking Time: None

Ingredients:
- 3 tablespoons red wine vinegar
- 3 tablespoons olive oil
- 1 tablespoon Dijon mustard
- Salt and pepper
- 8 cups fresh chopped romaine
- ¼ cup thinly sliced red onion
- 1 cup diced tomatoes
- 1 cup diced cucumber
- 4 ounces smoked turkey, sliced
- 4 slices turkey bacon, cooked and chopped
- 4 large hardboiled eggs, peeled and sliced

Directions:
1. Whisk together the vinegar, olive oil, mustard, salt, and pepper in a small bowl.
2. Divide the lettuce, red onion, tomatoes, and cucumber among four salad plates.
3. Top each with ¼ of the turkey and turkey bacon.
4. Add a sliced egg to each salad and drizzle with dressing to serve.

Nutrition:
- Info Calories 390,Total Fat 14.1gSaturated Fat 3.3g, Total Carbs 48.2g, Net Carbs 34.8g,Protein 20.3g,Sugar 3.2 Fiber 13.4g, Sodium 207mg

Crispy Baked Tofu

Servings: 4
Cooking Time: 25 Minutes

Ingredients:
- 1 (14-ounce) block extra-firm tofu
- 1 tablespoon olive oil
- 1 tablespoon cornstarch
- ½ teaspoon garlic powder
- Salt and pepper

Directions:
1. Lay some paper towels out on a flat surface.
2. Cut the tofu into slices up to about ½-inch thick and lay them out.
3. Cover the tofu with another paper towel and place a cutting board on top.
4. Let the tofu drain for 10 to 15 minutes.
5. Preheat the oven to 400°F and line a baking sheet with foil or parchment.
6. Cut the tofu into cubes and place in a large bowl.
7. Toss with the olive oil, cornstarch, and garlic powder, salt and pepper until coated.
8. Spread on the baking sheet and bake for 10 minutes.
9. Flip the tofu and bake for another 10 to 15 minutes until crisp. Servings:hot.

Nutrition:
- Info Calories 140 Total Fat 8.7g,Saturated Fat 1.1g, Total Carbs 2.1g, Net Carbs 2g,Protein.7g, Sugar 0.1g, Fiber 0.1g, Sodium 23mg

Quick And Easy Shrimp Stir-fry

Servings: 5
Cooking Time: 15 Minutes

Ingredients:

- 1 tablespoon olive oil
- 1 pound uncooked shrimp, peeled and deveined
- Salt and pepper
- 1 tablespoon sesame oil
- 8 ounces snow peas
- 4 ounces broccoli, chopped
- 1 medium red pepper, sliced
- 3 cloves minced garlic
- 1 tablespoon fresh grated ginger
- ½ cup soy sauce
- 1 tablespoon cornstarch
- 2 tablespoons fresh lime juice
- ¼ teaspoon liquid stevia extract

Directions:

1. Heat the olive oil in a large skillet over medium heat.
2. Add the shrimp and season with salt and pepper then sauté until just pink, about 5 minutes.
3. Remove the shrimp to a bowl and keep warm.
4. Reheat the skillet with the sesame oil and add the veggies.
5. Sauté until the veggies are tender, about 6 to 8 minutes.
6. Stir in the garlic and ginger and cook for 1 minute more.
7. Whisk together the remaining ingredients and pour into the skillet.
8. Toss to coat the veggies then add the shrimp and reheat. Servings:hot.

Nutrition:

- Info Calories 220, Total Fat 7.4g, Saturated Fat 1.3g, Total Carbs 12.7g,Net Carbs 10.1g,Protein 24.8g, Sugar 3.9g, Fiber 2.6g, Sodium 1670mg

Asian Cold Noodle Salad

Servings: 1
Cooking Time: None

Ingredients:

- 3 tablespoons light coconut milk
- 2 tablespoons whipped peanut butter
- 1 tablespoon water
- 1 tablespoon fresh lime juice
- ½ tablespoon soy sauce
- ¼ to ½ teaspoon sriracha sauce
- 1 ounce whole-wheat spaghetti, cooked
- ½ cup snow peas, halved
- 2 ounces cooked chicken breast, chopped
- ¼ cup diced red pepper
- 1 teaspoon fresh chopped cilantro
- 1 green onion, sliced thin

Directions:

1. Stir together the coconut milk, peanut butter, water, lime juice, soy sauce, and sriracha sauce in a small bowl.
2. Cook the spaghetti to al dente then drain and rinse under cool water.
3. Combine the cooled spaghetti, snow peas, chicken, red pepper, and cilantro in a bowl.
4. Toss with the dressing until well coated then serve with sliced green onion.

Nutrition:

- Info Calories 375, Total Fat 15gSaturated Fat 3.1g, Total Carbs 36.3g, Net Carbs 28.2g,Protein 26.2g, Sugar 8.3g, Fiber 8.1g, Sodium 627mg

Turkey & Brown Rice Lettuce Cups

Servings: 4

Cooking Time: 15 Minutes

Ingredients:

- ½ cup water
- ½ cup instant brown rice
- 1 tablespoon sesame oil
- 1 pound 93% lean ground turkey
- 1 tablespoon fresh grated ginger
- 1 medium red pepper, diced
- ½ cup fat-free chicken broth
- 1 ½ tablespoons soy sauce
- 1 teaspoon Chinese 5-spice powder
- Salt to taste
- 2 heads Boston lettuce, leaves separated
- Shredded carrot, to serve
- Fresh cilantro, to serve

Directions:

1. Bring the water to boil in a small saucepan then stir in the rice.
2. Reduce heat to low and cook, covered, for 5 minutes then set aside off the heat.
3. Heat the oil in a large skillet over medium-high heat and add the turkey and ginger.
4. Cook for 5 minutes, crumbling the turkey with a spoon.
5. Stir in the cooked rice along with the peppers, broth, soy sauce, spices, and salt.
6. Cook for 1 minute until heated through.
7. Spoon the turkey and brown rice mixture into lettuce cups.
8. Garnish with shredded carrot and cilantro to serve.

Nutrition:

- Info Calories 270, Total Fat 12.1gSaturated Fat 3g,Total Carbs 14.7g, Net Carbs 12.3g, Protein 24g, Sugar 4.1gFiber 2.4g, Sodium 529mg

Beef Fajitas

Servings: 4
Cooking Time: 15 Minutes

Ingredients:

- 1 lbs. lean beef sirloin, sliced thin
- 1 tablespoon olive oil
- 1 medium red onion, sliced
- 1 red pepper, sliced thin
- 1 green pepper, sliced thin
- ½ teaspoon ground cumin
- ½ teaspoon chili powder
- 8 (6-inch) whole-wheat tortillas
- Fat-free sour cream

Directions:

1. Heat a large cast-iron skillet over medium heat then add the oil.
2. Add the sliced beef and cook in a single layer for 1 minute on each side.
3. Remove the beef to a bowl and cover to keep warm.
4. Reheat the skillet then add the onions and peppers – season with cumin and chili powder.
5. Stir-fry the veggies to your liking then add to the bowl with the beef.

Nutrition:

- Info Calories 430, Total Fat 14.8g, Saturated Fat 3.2g, Total Carbs 30.5g, Net Carbs 12.9g, Protein 41.2g, Sugar 3.4g, Fiber 17.6g, Sodium 561mg

Stir-fried Steak And Cabbage

Servings: 4
Cooking Time: 15

Ingredients:
- ½-pound sirloin steak, cut into strips
- 2 teaspoons cornstarch
- 1-tablespoon peanut oil
- 2 cups chopped red or green cabbage
- 1 yellow bell pepper, chopped
- 2 green onions, chopped
- 2 cloves garlic, sliced
- ½-cup commercial stir-fry sauce

Directions:
1. Toss the steak with the cornstarch and set aside
2. In a 6-inch metal bowl, combine the peanut oil with the cabbage. Place in the basket and cook for 3 to 4 minutes.
3. Remove the bowl from the basket and add the steak, pepper, onions, and garlic. Return to the air fryer and cook for 3 to 5 minutes or until the steak is cooked to desired doneness and vegetables are crisp and tender.
4. Add the stir-fry sauce and cook for 2 to 4 minutes or until hot. Servings:over rice.

Nutrition:
- Info Calories: 180; Total Fat: 7g; Saturated Fat: 2g; Cholesterol: 51mg; Sodium: 1,843mg;Carbohydrates: 9g; Fiber: 2g; Protein: 20g

BEEF, PORK & LAMB RECIPES

Chicken Tuscany

Servings: 4
Cooking Time: 15 Minutes

Ingredients:
- 1½ lbs. chicken breasts, boneless, skinless and sliced thin
- 1 cup spinach, chopped
- 1 cup half-n-half
- What you'll need from store cupboard:
- ½ cup reduced fat parmesan cheese
- ½ cup low sodium chicken broth
- ½ cup sun dried tomatoes
- 2 tbsp. olive oil
- 1 tsp Italian seasoning
- 1 tsp garlic powder

Directions:
1. Heat oil in a large skillet over med-high heat. Add chicken and cook 3-5 minutes per side, or until browned and cooked through. Transfer to a plate.
2. Add half-n-half, broth, cheese and seasonings to the pan. Whisk constantly until sauce starts to thicken. Add spinach and tomatoes and cook, stirring frequently, until spinach starts to wilt, about 2-3 minutes.
3. Add chicken back to the pan and cook just long enough to heat through.

Nutrition:
- InfoCalories 462 Total Carbs 6g Net Carbs 5g Protein 55g Fat 23g Sugar 0g Fiber 1g

Creamy Turkey & Peas With Noodles

Servings: 4

Cooking Time: 15 Minutes

Ingredients:

- 1 lb. lean ground turkey
- 1 lemon, juice and zest
- 1 ½ cup skim milk
- 1 cup low fat sharp cheddar cheese, grated
- 1 cup peas, frozen
- ¼ cup fresh parsley, diced
- 1 tbsp. margarine
- What you'll need from store cupboard:
- Homemade noodles, (chapter 14)
- ½ cup low sodium chicken broth
- 3 tbsp. flour
- 1 tbsp. olive oil
- 3 cloves garlic, diced fine
- ½ tsp ground mustard
- Pinch of nutmeg
- Salt and pepper, to taste

Directions:

1. Heat oil in a large skillet over med-high heat. Add turkey and season with salt and pepper. Cook, breaking up with a spatula, until no longer pink. Add garlic and cook 1 minute more.
2. Add the margarine and flour, and cook, stirring, 2 minutes until combined.
3. Stir in the broth and milk. Bring to a low boil, reduce heat to low and simmer until mixture starts to thicken.
4. Add the cheese and cook, stirring until it melts and combines into the sauce. Add the seasonings and peas, simmer 5 minutes, stirring occasionally.
5. Add the noodles and lemon juice and cook another 2 minutes. Serve garnished with lemon zest and parsley.

Nutrition:

- InfoCalories 427 Total Carbs 18g Net Carbs 16g Protein 40g Fat 22g Sugar 7g Fiber 2g

Potatoes With Loin And Cheese(2)

Servings: 4
Cooking Time: 30 Minutes

Ingredients:
- 1kg of potatoes
- 1 large onion
- 1 piece of roasted loin
- Extra virgin olive oil
- Salt
- Ground pepper
- Grated cheese

Directions:
1. Peel the potatoes, cut the cane, wash, and dry.
2. Put salt and add some threads of oil, bind well.
3. Pass the potatoes to the basket of the air fryer and select 1800C, 20 minutes.
4. Meanwhile, in a pan, put some extra virgin olive oil, add the peeled onion, and cut into julienne.
5. When the onion is transparent, add the chopped loin.
6. Sauté well and pepper.
7. Put the potatoes on a baking sheet.
8. Add the onion with the loin.
9. Cover with a layer of grated cheese.
10. Bake a little until the cheese takes heat and melts.

Nutrition:
- InfoCalories: 323 Fat: 3.41g Carbohydrates: 0g Protein: 20.99g Sugar: 0gCholesterol: 0mg

Crock Pot Beef Roast With Gravy

Servings: 10
Cooking Time: 5 ½ Hours

Ingredients:
- 3 lb. beef sirloin tip roast
- What you'll need from store cupboard:
- ¼ cup lite soy sauce
- ¼ cup water
- 3 tbsp. balsamic vinegar
- 2 tbsp. cornstarch
- 2 tbsp. coarse ground pepper
- 1 tbsp. Worcestershire sauce
- 2 tsp ground mustard
- 1 ½ tsp garlic, diced fine

Directions:
1. Rub roast with garlic and pepper. Cut in half and place in crock pot.
2. Combine soy sauce, vinegar, Worcestershire, and mustard, pour over roast.
3. Cover and cook on low heat 5 ½-6 hours or until beef is tender.
4. Remove roast and keep warm. Strain juices into a small sauce pan, skim off fat. Heat over medium heat.
5. Stir water and cornstarch together until smooth. Stir into beef juices. Bring to a boil, and cook, stirring, 2 minutes or until thickened. Serve with roast.

Nutrition:
- InfoCalories 264 Total Carbs 3g Protein 37g Fat 12g Sugar 0g Fiber 0g

Alfredo Sausage & Vegetables

Servings: 6
Cooking Time: 15 Minutes

Ingredients:
- 1 pkg. smoked sausage, cut in ¼-inch slices
- 1 cup half-and-half
- ½ cup zucchini, cut in matchsticks
- ½ cup carrots, cut in matchsticks
- ½ cup red bell pepper, cut in matchsticks
- ½ cup peas, frozen
- ¼ cup margarine
- ¼ cup onion, diced
- 2 tbsp. fresh parsley, diced
- What you'll need from store cupboard:
- ½ recipe Homemade Pasta, cook & drain, (chapter 15)
- 1/3 cup reduced fat parmesan cheese
- 1 clove garlic, diced fine
- Salt & pepper, to taste

Directions:
1. Melt margarine in a large skillet over medium heat. Add onion and garlic and cook, stirring occasionally, 3-4 minutes or until onion is soft.
2. Increase heat to med-high. Add sausage, zucchini, carrots, and red pepper. Cook, stirring frequently, 5-6 minutes, or until carrots are tender crisp.
3. Stir in peas and half-n-half, cook 1-2 minutes until heated through. Stir in cheese, parsley, salt, and pepper. Add pasta nd toss to mix. Serve.

Nutrition:
- InfoCalories 283 Total Carbs 18g Net Carbs 14g Protein 21g Fat 15g Sugar 8g Fiber 4g

Beef Scallops

Servings: 4
Cooking Time: 20 Minutes

Ingredients:
- 16 veal scallops
- Salt
- Ground pepper
- Garlic powder
- 2 eggs
- Breadcrumbs
- Extra virgin olive oil

Directions:
1. Put the beef scallops well spread, salt, and pepper. Add some garlic powder.
2. In a bowl, beat the eggs.
3. In another bowl put the breadcrumbs.
4. Pass the Beef scallops for beaten egg and then for the breadcrumbs.
5. Spray with extra virgin olive oil on both sides.
6. Put a batch in the basket of the air fryer. Do not pile the scallops too much.
7. Select 1800C, 15 minutes. From time to time, shake the basket so that the scallops move.
8. When finishing that batch, put the next one and so on until you finish with everyone, usually 4 or 5 scallops enter per batch.

Nutrition:
- InfoCalories: 330 Fat: 3.41g Carbohydrates: 0g Protein: 20.99g Sugar: 0gCholesterol:1 65mg

Pork Trinoza Wrapped In Ham

Servings: 6
Cooking Time: 20 Minutes

Ingredients:

- 6 pieces of Serrano ham, thinly sliced
- 454g pork, halved, with butter and crushed
- 6g of salt
- 1g black pepper
- 227g fresh spinach leaves, divided
- 4 slices of mozzarella cheese, divided
- 18g sun-dried tomatoes, divided
- 10 ml of olive oil, divided

Directions:

1. Place 3 pieces of ham on baking paper, slightly overlapping each other. Place 1 half of the pork in the ham. Repeat with the other half.
2. Season the inside of the pork rolls with salt and pepper.
3. Place half of the spinach, cheese, and sun-dried tomatoes on top of the pork loin, leaving a 13 mm border on all sides.
4. Roll the fillet around the filling well and tie with a kitchen cord to keep it closed.
5. Repeat the process for the other pork steak and place them in the fridge.
6. Select Preheat in the air fryer and press Start/Pause.
7. Brush 5 ml of olive oil on each wrapped steak and place them in the preheated air fryer.
8. Select Steak. Set the timer to 9 minutes and press Start/Pause.
9. Allow it to cool for 10 minutes before cutting.

Nutrition:

- InfoCalories: 282 Fat: 23.41 Carbohydrates: 0g Protein: 16.59 Sugar: 0g Cholesterol: 73gm

Roast Turkey & Rosemary Gravy

Servings: 18

Cooking Time: 1 ¾ Hours

Ingredients:

- 6 lb. turkey breast, bone in
- 2 apples, sliced
- 1 ½ cup leek, sliced, white parts only
- 3 tbsp. margarine
- 2 tsp fresh rosemary, diced, divided
- What you'll need from store cupboard:
- 2 ¼ cup low sodium chicken broth
- ¼ cup flour
- 1 tbsp. sunflower oil

Directions:

1. Heat oven to 325 degrees.
2. Place apples and leeks in the bottom of a large roasting pan, and pour in 1 cup of broth. Place turkey on top.
3. In a small bowl, combine oil and 1 ½ teaspoons rosemary. Loosen skin over turkey and rub rosemary mixture over the turkey. Secure skin to underside of turkey with toothpicks.
4. Bake 1 ¾-2 ¼ hours, basting every 30 minutes, until turkey is cooked through. If turkey starts to get too brown, cover with foil.
5. Once turkey is done, cover and let rest 15 minutes before slicing. Discard apples and leeks. Save ¼ cup cooking liquid.
6. Melt margarine in a small saucepan over medium heat. Add flour and remaining rosemary and cook, stirring, until combined. Skim fat off the reserved cooking liquid and add to saucepan with remaining broth. Bring to a boil, cook, stirring, 1 minute until thickened. Serve with turkey.

Nutrition:

- InfoCalories 306 Total Carbs 6g Net Carbs 5g Protein 33g Fat 14g Sugar 3g Fiber 1g

Pork Loin With Onion Beer Sauce

Servings: 6

Cooking Time: 3 Hours

Ingredients:

- 1 ½ lb. pork loin
- 1 ½ cup dark beer
- 1 large onion, sliced
- What you'll need from store cupboard:
- 2 cloves garlic, diced fine
- 3 tbsp. water
- 2 tbsp. cornstarch
- 1 tbsp. olive oil
- 1 tbsp. Dijon mustard
- 2 bay leaves

Directions:

1. Heat oil in a large skillet over med-high heat. Add onions and cook until tender. Add the pork and brown on all sides. Transfer to the crock pot.
2. Add the beer, mustard, garlic, and bay leaves. Cover and cook on high 3 hours, or until pork is tender.
3. Transfer pork to a plate. Whisk together the corn starch and water and add to the crock pot, stir well. Let cook until sauce thickens, about 30 minutes.
4. Slice the pork and serve topped with sauce.

Nutrition:

- InfoCalories 342 Total Carbs 7g Protein 31g Fat 18g Sugar 1g Fiber 0g

Beef Patty

Servings: 4
Cooking Time: 30 Minutes

Ingredients:
- Prepared dough
- 300g beef
- 1 large onion
- 1 red pepper
- 2 hard-boiled eggs
- Salt
- Pepper to taste.
- 1 tsp. oil

Directions:
1. Remove the dough from the refrigerator 10 minutes before.
2. In a pan, place oil, 1 onion, 1 pepper, garlic, seasoning. Add ground beef until cooked well. Season with salt and pepper to taste.
3. Let the filling cool
4. Place the filling in each circle of the dough and seal with egg white at the edges.
5. Butter a refractory mold and accommodate the patty.
6. Preheat the oven to 190°C for 10 minutes by pressing the Convection button
7. Place the refractory on the metal rack and bring to the preheated oven for 30 minutes at 190°C.

Nutrition:
- InfoCalories: 269 Fat: 3.41g Carbohydrates: 0g Protein: 20.99g Sugar: 0gCholesterol: 25mg

Cashew Chicken

Servings: 4
Cooking Time: 10 Minutes

Ingredients:

- 1 lb. skinless boneless chicken breast, cut in cubes
- 1/2 onion, sliced
- 2 tbsp. green onion, diced
- ½ tsp fresh ginger, peeled and grated
- What you'll need from store cupboard:
- 1 cup whole blanched cashews, toasted
- 1 clove garlic, diced fine
- 4 tbsp. oil
- 2 tbsp. dark soy sauce
- 2 tbsp. hoisin sauce
- 2 tbsp. water
- 2 tsp cornstarch
- 2 tsp dry sherry
- 1 tsp Splenda
- 1 tsp sesame seed oil

Directions:

1. Place chicken in a large bowl and add cornstarch, sherry, and ginger. Stir until well mixed.
2. In a small bowl, whisk together soy sauce, hoisin, Splenda, and water stirring until smooth.
3. Heat the oil in a wok or a large skillet over high heat. Add garlic and onion and cook, stirring until garlic sizzles, about 30 seconds.
4. Stir in chicken and cook, stirring frequently, until chicken is almost done, about 2 minutes.
5. Reduce heat to medium and stir in sauce mixture. Continue cooking and stirring until everything is blended together. Add cashews and cook 30 seconds.
6. Drizzle with sesame oil, and cook another 30 seconds, stirring constantly. Serve immediately garnished with green onions.

Nutrition:

- InfoCalories 483 Total Carbs 19g Net Carbs 17g Protein 33g Fat 32g Sugar 6g Fiber 2g

Chicken's Liver

Servings: 4
Cooking Time: 30 Minutes

Ingredients:

- 500g of chicken livers
- 2 or 3 carrots
- 1 green pepper
- 1 red pepper
- 1 onion
- 4 tomatoes
- Salt
- Ground pepper
- 1 glass of white wine
- ½ glass of water
- Extra virgin olive oil

Directions:

1. Peel the carrots, cut them into slices and add them to the bowl of the air fryer with a tablespoon of extra virgin olive oil 5 minutes.
2. After 5 minutes, add the peppers and onion in julienne. Select 5 minutes.
3. After that time, add the tomatoes in wedges and select 5 more minutes.
4. Add now the chicken liver clean and chopped.
5. Season, add the wine and water.
6. Select 10 minutes.
7. Check that the liver is tender.

Nutrition:

- Info 76 Fat: 13g Carbohydrates: 1g Protein: 2Sugar: 1gCholesterol: 130mg

FISH AND SEAFOOD RECIPES

Italian Steamed Mussels

Servings: 4
Cooking Time: 10 Minutes

Ingredients:
- 2 lbs. mussels, cleaned
- 2 plum tomatoes, peeled, seeded and diced
- 1 cup onion, diced
- 2 tbsp. fresh parsley, diced
- What you'll need from store cupboard:
- ¼ cup dry white wine
- 3 cloves garlic, diced fine
- 3 tbsp. olive oil
- 2 tbsp. fresh breadcrumbs
- ¼ teaspoon crushed red pepper flakes

Directions:
1. Heat oil in a large sauce pot over medium heat. Add the onions and cook until soft, about 2-3 minutes. Add garlic and cook 1 minute more.
2. Stir in wine, tomatoes, and pepper flakes. Bring to a boil, stirring occasionally. Add the mussels and cook 3-4 minutes, or until all the mussels have opened. Discard any mussels that do not open.
3. Once mussels open, transfer them to a serving bowl. Add bread crumbs to the sauce and continue to cook, stirring frequently, until mixture thickens. Stir in parsley and pour evenly over mussels. Serve.

Nutrition:
- InfoCalories 340 Total Carbs 18g Net Carbs 16g Protein 29g Fat 16g Sugar 4g Fiber 2g

Tuna Carbonara

Servings: 4
Cooking Time: 25 Minutes

Ingredients:

- ½ lb. tuna fillet, cut in pieces
- 2 eggs
- 4 tbsp. fresh parsley, diced
- What you'll need from store cupboard:
- ½ recipe Homemade Pasta, cook & drain, (chapter 15)
- ½ cup reduced fat parmesan cheese
- 2 cloves garlic, peeled
- 2 tbsp. extra virgin olive oil
- Salt & pepper, to taste

Directions:

1. In a small bowl, beat the eggs, parmesan and a dash of pepper.
2. Heat the oil in a large skillet over med-high heat. Add garlic and cook until browned. Add the tuna and cook 2-3 minutes, or until tuna is almost cooked through. Discard the garlic.
3. Add the pasta and reduce heat. Stir in egg mixture and cook, stirring constantly, 2 minutes. If the sauce is too thick, thin with water, a little bit at a time, until it has a creamy texture.
4. Salt and pepper to taste and serve garnished with parsley.

Nutrition:

- InfoCalories 409 Total Carbs 7g Net Carbs 6g Protein 25g Fat 30g Sugar 3g Fiber 1g

Shrimp With Pumpkin Risotto

Servings: 3
Cooking Time: 15 Minutes

Ingredients:

- ½ lb. raw shrimp, peel & devein
- 2 cups cauliflower, grated
- ¼ cup half-n-half
- 2 tbsp. margarine
- What you'll need from store cupboard:
- ½ cup low sodium vegetable broth
- ¼ cup pumpkin puree
- ¼ cup reduced fat parmesan cheese
- 2 cloves garlic, diced fine
- ¼ tsp sage
- ¼ tsp salt
- ¼ tsp pepper

Directions:

1. Melt margarine in a large skillet over med-high heat. Add garlic and cook 1-2 minutes.
2. Add the broth, pumpkin, and half-n-half and whisk until smooth.
3. Add cauliflower and parmesan and cook 5 minutes, or until cauliflower is tender. Stir in shrimp and cook until they turn pink. Season with salt and pepper and serve.

Nutrition:

- InfoCalories 236 Total Carbs 9g Net Carbs 7g Protein 21g Fat 13g Sugar 3g Fiber 2g

Paella

Servings: 6
Cooking Time: 35 Minutes

Ingredients:

- 1 lb. chicken thighs, skinless & boneless
- 1 lb. medium shrimp, raw, peel & devein
- 1 dozen mussels, cleaned
- 2 chorizo sausages, cut into pieces
- 1 medium head cauliflower, grated
- 1 yellow onion, diced fine
- 1 green bell pepper, sliced into strips
- 1 cup frozen peas
- What you'll need from store cupboard:
- 15 oz. can tomatocs, diced, drain well
- 2 tbsp. extra-virgin olive oil
- 2 tsp garlic, diced fine
- 2 tsp salt
- 1 tsp saffron
- ½ tsp pepper
- ¼ tsp paprika
- Nonstick cooking spray

Directions:

1. Heat the oven to broil. Spray a baking dish with cooking spray.
2. Sprinkle salt and pepper on both sides of the chicken and place in baking dish. Bake, about 4 minutes per side, until no longer pink in the middle. Let cool completely.
3. Heat 1 tablespoon of the oil in a medium skillet over medium heat. Add onion, pepper, and garlic. Cook, about 4-5 minutes, stirring frequently, until peppers start to get soft. Transfer to a bowl.
4. Add chorizo to the skillet and cook 2 minutes, stirring frequently. Drain off the fat and add to the vegetables.
5. Once the chicken has cooled, cut into small pieces and add it to the vegetables.
6. In a large saucepot, over medium heat, add the remaining oil. Once it is hot, add the cauliflower and seasonings. Cook 8-10 minutes, until cauliflower is almost tender, stirring frequently.
7. Add the mussels and shrimp and cook until mussels open and shrimp start to turn pink.
8. Add the mixture in the bowl with the tomatoes and peas and stir to combine everything together. Cook another 5 minutes until everything is heated through and all of the mussels have opened. Serve.

Nutrition:

- InfoCalories 423 Total Carbs 21g Net Carbs 15g Protein 46g Fat 18g Sugar 9g Fiber 6g

Pan Seared Trout & Salsa

Servings: 6
Cooking Time: 10 Minutes

Ingredients:
- 6 6 oz. trout filets
- 6 lemon slices
- What you'll need from store cupboard:
- 4 tbsp. olive oil
- ¾ tsp salt
- ½ tsp pepper
- Italian-Style Salsa, (chapter 16)

Directions:
1. Sprinkle filets with salt and pepper.
2. Heat oil in a large nonstick skillet over med-high heat. Cook trout, 3 filets at a time, 2-3 minutes per side, or fish flakes easily with a fork. Repeat with remaining filets.
3. Serve topped with salsa and a slice of lemon.

Nutrition:
- InfoCalories 320 Total Carbs 2g Protein 30g Fat 21g Sugar 1g Fiber 0g

Jambalaya

Servings: 6
Cooking Time: 40 Minutes

Ingredients:

- 1 lb. raw shrimp, peel & devein
- 14 oz. Andouille sausage, cut into 1-inch pieces
- 1 medium cauliflower, riced
- 4 stalks celery, diced
- ½ white onion, diced
- ½ red bell pepper, diced
- 4 tbsp. margarine
- What you'll need from store cupboard:
- 2 cups low sodium chicken broth
- ½ can tomatoes & green chilies
- 3 cloves garlic, diced fine
- 2 tsp garlic powder
- 2 tsp Old Bay
- 1 ½ tsp onion powder
- 1 tsp thyme
- 1 tsp oregano
- 1 tsp basil
- 1/2 tsp cayenne pepper

Directions:

1. Place large stock pot over med-high heat.
2. In a small bowl, stir together garlic powder, onion powder, thyme, oregano, basil, Old Bay, and cayenne until combined.
3. Add 2 tablespoons margarine to the stock pot and let melt.
4. Add the riced cauliflower with 2 teaspoons of the spice mixture. Cook, stirring frequently, about 5 minutes. Transfer to a bowl.
5. Add the remaining margarine to the stock pot and melt. Then add the sausage and cook 5 minutes, stirring to brown all sides.
6. Add onion, celery, and pepper and stir to combine. Cook about 3 minutes until vegetables start to get soft.
7. Add the garlic and cook, stirring, 1 minute. Add the cauliflower and combine then add half the spice mixture and tomatoes, simmer 2-3 minutes.
8. Pour in the broth and bring to a boil, cook 8-10 minutes.
9. Season shrimp with remaining spice mixture and add to the pot, cook 3-4 minutes just until shrimp turn pink. Serve.

Nutrition:

- InfoCalories 428 Total Carbs 13g Net Carbs 10g Protein 33g Fat 27g Sugar 4g Fiber 3g

Salmon Milano

Servings: 6
Cooking Time: 20 Minutes

Ingredients:
- 2 ½ lb. salmon filet
- 2 tomatoes, sliced
- ½ cup margarine
- What you'll need from store cupboard:
- ½ cup basil pesto

Directions:
1. Heat the oven to 400 degrees. Line a 9x15-inch baking sheet with foil, making sure it covers the sides. Place another large piece of foil onto the baking sheet and place the salmon filet on top of it.
2. Place the pesto and margarine in blender or food processor and pulse until smooth. Spread evenly over salmon. Place tomato slices on top.
3. Wrap the foil around the salmon, tenting around the top to prevent foil from touching the salmon as much as possible. Bake 15-25 minutes, or salmon flakes easily with a fork. Serve.

Nutrition:
- InfoCalories 444 Total Carbs 2g Protein 55g Fat 24g Sugar 1g Fiber 0g

Grilled Tuna Steaks

Servings: 6
Cooking Time: 10 Minutes

Ingredients:

- 6 6 oz. tuna steaks
- 3 tbsp. fresh basil, diced
- What you'll need from store cupboard:
- 4 ½ tsp olive oil
- ¾ tsp salt
- ¼ tsp pepper
- Nonstick cooking spray

Directions:

1. Heat grill to medium heat. Spray rack with cooking spray.
2. Drizzle both sides of the tuna with oil. Sprinkle with basil, salt and pepper.
3. Place on grill and cook 5 minutes per side, tuna should be slightly pink in the center. Serve.

Nutrition:

- InfoCalories 343 Total Carbs 0g Protein 51g Fat 14g Sugar 0g Fiber 0g

Tangy Orange Roughy

Servings: 4
Cooking Time: 15 Minutes

Ingredients:

- 4 orange roughy filets
- ¼ cup fresh lemon juice
- What you'll need from store cupboard:
- ¼ cup reduced sodium soy sauce
- 1 tbsp. Splenda
- ½ tsp ginger
- ½ tsp lemon pepper
- Nonstick cooking spray

Directions:

1. In a large Ziploc bag combine lemon juice, soy sauce, Splenda, and ginger. Add fish, seal, and turn to coat. Refrigerate 30 minutes.
2. Heat oven to 350 degrees. Spray a large baking sheet with cooking spray.
3. Place filets on prepared pan and sprinkle with lemon pepper. Bake 12-15 minutes, or until fish flakes easily with fork.

Nutrition:

- InfoCalories 239 Total Carbs 4g Net Carbs 3g Protein 25g Fat 12g Sugar 4g Fiber 1g

Crab Cakes

Servings: 8 (2 Crab Cakes Per Serving)
Cooking Time: 10 Minutes

Ingredients:
- 1 lb. lump blue crabmeat
- 1 tbsp. red bell pepper, diced fine
- 1 tbsp. green bell pepper, diced fine
- 1 tbsp. fresh parsley, chopped fine
- 2 eggs
- ¼ tsp fresh lemon juice
- What you'll need from store cupboard:
- ¼ cup + 1 tbsp. lite mayonnaise
- ¼ cup Dijon mustard
- 2 tbsp. sunflower oil
- 1 tbsp. baking powder
- 1 tbsp. Worcestershire sauce
- 1 ½ tsp Old Bay

Directions:
1. In a small bowl, whisk together ¼ cup mayonnaise, Dijon mustard, Worcestershire, and lemon juice until combined. Cover and chill until ready to serve.
2. In a large bowl, mix crab, bell peppers, parsley, eggs, 1 tablespoon mayonnaise, baking powder, and Old Bay seasoning until Ingredients are combined.
3. Heat oil in a large skillet over med-high heat. Once oil is hot, drop 2 tablespoons crab mixture into hot skillet. They will be loose but as the egg cooks they will hold together.
4. Cook 2 minutes or until firm, then flip and cook another minutes. Transfer to serving plate. Serve with mustard dipping sauce.

Nutrition:
- InfoCalories 96 Total Carbs 3g Protein 12g Fat 4g Sugar 1g Fiber 0g

Broiled Teriyaki Salmon

Servings:4
Cooking Time: 3 To 5 Minutes

Ingredients:
- ⅓ cup low-sodium soy sauce
- ⅓ cup pineapple juice
- ¼ cup water
- 2 tablespoons rice vinegar
- 1 garlic clove, minced
- 1 tablespoon honey
- 1 teaspoon peeled and grated fresh ginger
- Pinch red pepper flakes
- 1 pound (454 g) salmon fillet, cut into 4 pieces

Directions:
1. Preheat the oven broiler on high.
2. Stir together the soy sauce, pineapple juice, water, vinegar, garlic, honey, ginger, and red pepper flakes in a small bowl.
3. Marinate the fillets (flesh-side down) in the sauce for about 5 minutes.
4. Transfer the fillets (flesh-side up) to a rimmed baking sheet and brush them generously with any leftover sauce.
5. Broil the fish until it flakes apart easily and reaches an internal temperature of 145°F (63°C), about 3 to 5 minutes.
6. Let the fish cool for 5 minutes before serving.

Nutrition:
- Infocalories: 201 | fat: 6.8g | protein: 23.7g | carbs: 8.9g | fiber: 1.0g | sugar: 10.2g| sodium: 750mg

Shrimp Coleslaw

Servings:4
Cooking Time: 0 Minutes

Ingredients:
- 1 pound (454 g) frozen cooked shrimp, thawed
- 1 (8-ounce / 227-g) package shredded cabbage
- 3 tangerines, peeled and sectioned
- 3 scallions, sliced
- 3 tablespoons olive oil
- 2 teaspoons grated fresh ginger root
- 2 tablespoons white rice vinegar
- ⅛ teaspoon red pepper flakes
- 1 avocado, peeled, pitted, and sliced
- ¼ cup toasted slivered almonds (optional)
- 3 tablespoons chopped fresh cilantro

Directions:
1. Stir together the shrimp, cabbage, tangerines, scallions, olive oil, ginger root, vinegar, and red pepper flakes in a large bowl.
2. Transfer to the refrigerator to chill for at least 30 minutes.
3. When ready to serve, sprinkle the avocado slices, almonds (if desired), and cilantro on top. Serve immediately.

Nutrition:
- Infocalories: 362 | fat: 18.1g | protein: 29.6g | carbs: 20.5g | fiber: 5.4g | sugar: 8.3g| sodium: 138mg

Red Clam Sauce & Pasta

Servings: 4
Cooking Time: 3 Hours

Ingredients:
- 1 onion, diced
- ¼ cup fresh parsley, diced
- What you'll need from store cupboard:
- 2 6 ½ oz. cans clams, chopped, undrained
- 14 ½ oz. tomatoes, diced, undrained
- 6 oz. tomato paste
- 2 cloves garlic, diced
- 1 bay leaf
- 1 tbsp. sunflower oil
- 1 tsp Splenda
- 1 tsp basil
- ½ tsp thyme
- ½ recipe Homemade Pasta, cook & drain (chapter 15)

Directions:
1. Heat oil in a small skillet over med-high heat. Add onion and cook until tender, Add garlic and cook 1 minute more. Transfer to crock pot.
2. Add remaining Ingredients, except pasta, cover and cook on low 3-4 hours.
3. Discard bay leaf and serve over cooked pasta.

Nutrition:
- InfoCalories 223 Total Carbs 32g Net Carbs 27g Protein 12g Fat 6g Sugar 15g Fiber 5g

MEATLESS RECIPES

Vegetables In Air Fryer

Servings: 2
Cooking Time: 30 Minutes

Ingredients:
- 2 potatoes
- 1 zucchini
- 1 onion
- 1 red pepper
- 1 green pepper

Directions:
1. Cut the potatoes into slices.
2. Cut the onion into rings.
3. Cut the zucchini slices
4. Cut the peppers into strips.
5. Put all the ingredients in the bowl and add a little salt, ground pepper and some extra virgin olive oil.
6. Mix well.
7. Pass to the basket of the air fryer.
8. Select 1600C, 30 minutes.
9. Check that the vegetables are to your liking.

Nutrition:
- Info Calories: 135Cal Carbs: 2 g Fat: 11 g Protein: 4 g Fiber: 05g

Holiday Apple & Cranberry Salad

Servings: 10
Cooking Time: 15 Minutes

Ingredients:

- 12 oz. salad greens
- 3 Honeycrisp apples, sliced thin
- 1/2 lemon
- ½ cup blue cheese, crumbled
- What you'll need from store cupboard:
- Apple Cider Vinaigrette (chapter 16)
- 1 cup pecan halves, toasted
- ¾ cup dried cranberries

Directions:

1. Put the apple slices in a large plastic bag and squeeze the half lemon over them. Close the bag and shake to coat.
2. In a large bowl, layer greens, apples, pecans, cranberries, and blue cheese. Just before serving, drizzle with enough vinaigrette to dress the salad. Toss to coat all Ingredients evenly.

Nutrition:

- InfoCalories 291 Total Carbs 19g Net Carbs 15g Protein 5g Fat 23g Sugar 13g Fiber 4g

Grilled Vegetable & Noodle Salad

Servings: 4
Cooking Time: 10 Minutes

Ingredients:

- 2 ears corn-on-the-cob, husked
- 1 red onion, cut in ½-inch thick slices
- 1 tomato, diced fine
- 1/3 cup fresh basil, diced
- 1/3 cup feta cheese, crumbled
- What you'll need from store cupboard:
- 1 recipe Homemade Noodles, (chapter 15) cook & drain
- 4 tbsp. Herb Vinaigrette, (chapter 16)
- Nonstick cooking spray

Directions:

1. Heat grill to medium heat. Spray rack with cooking spray.
2. Place corn and onions on the grill and cook, turning when needed, until lightly charred and tender, about 10 minutes.
3. Cut corn off the cob and place in a medium bowl. Chop the onion and add to the corn.
4. Stir in noodles, tomatoes, basil, and vinaigrette, toss to mix. Sprinkle cheese over top and serve.

Nutrition:

- InfoCalories 330 Total Carbs 19g Net Carbs 16g Protein 10g Fat 9g Sugar 5g Fiber 3g

Garden Vegetable Pasta

Servings: 6
Cooking Time: 30 Minutes

Ingredients:

- 2 lbs. fresh cherry tomatoes, halved
- 2 zucchini, chopped
- 2 ears corn, cut kernels off the cob
- 1 yellow squash, chopped
- ½ cup mozzarella cheese, grated
- ½ cup fresh basil, sliced thin
- What you'll need from store cupboard:
- Homemade Pasta, cook & drain, (chapter 15)
- 5 tbsp. olive oil, divided
- 2 cloves garlic crushed
- Crushed red pepper flakes, to taste
- Salt, to taste

Directions:

1. Heat 3 tablespoons oil in a large skillet over medium heat. Add garlic and tomatoes. Cover, reduce heat to low, and cook 15 minutes, stirring frequently.
2. In a separate skillet, heat remaining oil over med-high heat. Add zucchini, squash, and corn. Reduce heat to medium, and cook until vegetables are tender. Sprinkle with salt.
3. Heat oven to 400 degrees.
4. In a large bowl combine tomato mixture, vegetables, and pasta, toss to mix. Pour into a 9x13-inch baking dish and top with cheese. Bake 10 minutes, or until cheese melts and begins to brown. Serve.

Nutrition:

- InfoCalories 347 Total Carbs 31g Net Carbs 24g Protein 21g Fat 18g Sugar 13g Fiber 7g

Tex Mex Veggie Bake

Servings: 8
Cooking Time: 35 Minutes

Ingredients:
- 2 cup cauliflower, grated
- 1 cup fat free sour cream
- 1 cup reduced fat cheddar cheese, grated
- 1 cup reduced fat Mexican cheese blend, grated
- ½ cup red onion, diced
- What you'll need from store cupboard:
- 11 oz. can Mexicorn, drain
- 10 oz. tomatoes & green chilies
- 2 ¼ oz. black olives, drain
- 1 cup black beans, rinsed
- 1 cup salsa
- ¼ tsp pepper
- Nonstick cooking spray

Directions:
1. Heat oven to 350 degrees. Spray a 2 ½-quart baking dish with cooking spray.
2. In a large bowl, combine beans, corn, tomatoes, salsa, sour cream, cheddar cheese, pepper, and cauliflower. Transfer to baking dish. Sprinkle with onion and olives.
3. Bake 30 minutes. Sprinkle with Mexican blend cheese and bake another 5-10 minutes, or until cheese is melted and casserole is heated through. Let rest 10 minutes before serving.

Nutrition:
- InfoCalories 266 Total Carbs 33g Net Carbs 27g Protein 16g Fat 8g Sugar 8g Fiber 6g

Brussels Sprouts

Servings: 2
Cooking Time: 10 Minutes

Ingredients:
- 2 cups Brussels sprouts
- 1/4 teaspoon sea salt
- 1-tablespoon olive oil
- 1-tablespoon apple cider vinegar

Directions:
1. Switch on the air fryer, insert fryer basket, grease it with olive oil, then shut with its lid, set the fryer at 400 degrees F and preheat for 5 minutes.
2. Meanwhile, cut the sprouts lengthwise into ¼-inch thick pieces, add them in a bowl, add remaining ingredients and toss until well coated.
3. Open the fryer, add sprouts in it, close with its lid and cook for 10 minutes until crispy and cooked, shaking halfway through the frying.
4. When air fryer beeps, open its lid, transfer sprouts onto a serving plate and serve.

Nutrition:
- Info Calories: 88 Cal Carbs: 2 g Fat: 11 g Protein: 4 g Fiber: 4 g

Crock Pot Stroganoff

Servings: 2
Cooking Time: 2 Hours

Ingredients:

- 8 cups mushrooms, cut into quarters
- 1 onion, halved and sliced thin
- 4 tbsp. fresh parsley, chopped
- 1 ½ tbsp. low fat sour cream
- What you'll need from store cupboard:
- 1 cup low sodium vegetable broth
- 3 cloves garlic, diced fine
- 2 tsp smoked paprika
- Salt and pepper to taste

Directions:

1. Add all Ingredients, except sour cream and parsley to crock pot.cover and cook on high 2 hours.
2. Stir in sour cream and serve garnished with parsley.

Nutrition:

- InfoCalories 111 Total Carbs 18g Net Carbs 14g Protein 10g Fat 2g Sugar 8g Fiber 4g

Sautéed Zucchini And Tomatoes

Servings:4
Cooking Time: 10 Minutes

Ingredients:
- 1 tablespoon vegetable oil
- 1 sliced onion
- 2 pounds (907 g) zucchini, peeled and cut into 1-inch-thick slices
- 2 tomatoes, chopped
- 1 green bell pepper, chopped
- Salt and freshly ground black pepper, to taste

Directions:
1. Heat the vegetable oil in a nonstick skillet until it shimmers.
2. Sauté the onion slices in the oil for about 3 minutes until translucent, stirring occasionally.
3. Add the zucchini, tomatoes, bell pepper, salt, and pepper to the skillet and stir to combine.
4. Reduce the heat, cover, and continue cooking for about 5 minutes, or until the veggies are tender.
5. Remove from the heat to a large plate and serve hot.

Nutrition:
- Infocalories: 110 | fat: 4.4g | protein: 6.9g | carbs: 10.7g | fiber: 3.4g | sugar: 2.2g| sodium: 11mg

Broccoli & Bacon Salad

Servings: 4
Cooking Time:x

Ingredients:

- 2 cups broccoli, separated into florets
- 4 slices bacon, chopped and cooked crisp
- ½ cup cheddar cheese, cubed
- ¼ cup low-fat Greek yogurt
- 1/8 cup red onion, diced fine
- 1/8 cup almonds, sliced
- What you'll need from the store cupboard
- ¼ cup reduced-fat mayonnaise
- 1 tbsp. lemon juice
- 1 tbsp. apple cider vinegar
- 1 tbsp. granulated sugar substitute
- ¼ tsp salt
- ¼ tsp pepper

Directions:

1. In a large bowl, combine broccoli, onion, cheese, bacon, and almonds.
2. In a small bowl, whisk remaining Ingredients together till combined.
3. Pour dressing over broccoli mixture and stir. Cover and chill at least 1 hour before serving.

Nutrition:

- InfoCalories 217 Total Carbs 12g Net Carbs 10g Protein 11g Fat 14g Sugar 6g Fiber 2g

Shrimp & Avocado Salad

Servings: 4

Cooking Time: 5 Minutes

Ingredients:

- ½ lb. raw shrimp, peeled and deveined
- 3 cups romaine lettuce, chopped
- 1 cup napa cabbage, chopped
- 1 avocado, pit removed and sliced
- ¼ cup red cabbage, chopped
- 1/4 cucumber, julienned
- 2 tbsp. green onions, diced fine
- 2 tbsp. fresh cilantro, diced
- 1 tsp fresh ginger, diced fine
- What you'll need from the store cupboard
- 2 tbsp. coconut oil
- 1 tbsp. sesame seeds
- 1 tsp Chinese five spice
- Fat-free Ranch dressing

Directions:

1. Toast sesame seeds in a medium skillet over medium heat. Shake the skillet to prevent them from burning. Cook until they start to brown, about 2 minutes. Set aside.
2. Add the coconut oil to the skillet. Pat the shrimp dry and sprinkle with the five spice. Add to hot oil. Cook 2 minutes per side, or until they turn pink. Set aside.
3. Arrange lettuce and cabbage on a serving platter. Top with green onions, cucumber, and cilantro. Add shrimp and avocado.
4. Drizzle with desired amount of dressing and sprinkle sesame seeds over top. Serve.

Nutrition:

- InfoCalories 306 Total Carbs 20g Net Carbs 15g Protein 15g Fat 19g Sugar 4g Fiber 5g

Autumn Slaw

Servings: 8
Cooking Time: 2 Hours

Ingredients:

- 10 cup cabbage, shredded
- ½ red onion, diced fine
- ¾ cup fresh Italian parsley, chopped
- What you'll need from store cupboard:
- ¾ cup almonds, slice & toasted
- ¾ cup dried cranberries
- 1/3 cup vegetable oil
- ¼ cup apple cider vinegar
- 2 tbsp. sugar free maple syrup
- 4 tsp Dijon mustard
- ½ teaspoon salt
- Salt & pepper, to taste

Directions:

1. In a large bowl, whisk together vinegar, oil, syrup, Dijon, and ½ teaspoon salt. Add the onion and stir to combine. Let rest 10 minutes, or cover and refrigerate until ready to use.
2. After 10 minutes, add remaining Ingredients to the dressing mixture and toss to coat. Taste and season with salt and pepper if needed. Cover and chill 2 hours before serving.

Nutrition:

- InfoCalories 133   Total Carbs 12g net Carbs 8g Protein 2g Fat 9g Sugar 5g Fiber 4g

Fiesta Casserole

Servings: 12

Cooking Time: 30 Minutes

Ingredients:
- 1 head cauliflower, grated
- 1 red bell pepper, diced fine
- 1 green bell pepper, diced fine
- 1 jalapeno pepper, seeded and diced fine
- ½ white onion, diced fine
- 1½ cups cheddar cheese, grated
- 1 tsp cilantro, diced fine
- What you'll need from store cupboard:
- ½ cup salsa
- 3 tbsp. water
- 1 tsp chili powder
- Nonstick cooking spray

Directions:
1. Heat oven to 350 degrees. Spray a 7x11x2-inch baking pan with cooking spray.
2. In a large skillet, over medium heat, cook onions and peppers until soft, about 5 minutes. Add cilantro and chili powder and stir.
3. Place the cauliflower and water in a glass bowl and microwave on high for 3 minutes. Stir in 1 cup cheese and the salsa.
4. Stir the pepper mixture into the cauliflower and combine. Spread in prepared pan. Sprinkle the remaining cheese over the top and bake 30-35 minutes.
5. Let rest 5 minutes before cutting into 12 squares and serving.

Nutrition:
- al Facts Per ServingCalories 74 Total Carbs 4g Net Carbs 3g Protein 4g Fat 5g Sugar 2g Fiber 1g

Vegetables With Provolone

Servings: 4
Cooking Time: 30 Minutes

Ingredients:

- 1 bag of 400g of frozen tempura vegetables
- Extra virgin olive oil
- Salt
- 1 slice of provolone cheese

Directions:

1. Put the vegetables in the basket of the air fryer. Add some strands of extra virgin olive oil and close.
2. Select 20 minutes, 2000C.
3. Pass the vegetables to a clay pot and place the provolone cheese on top.
4. Take to the oven, 1800C, about 10 minutes or so or until you see that, the cheese has melted to your liking.

Nutrition:

- Info Calories: 104Cal Carbs: 2 g Fat: 11 g Protein: 4 g Fiber: 0 g

SNACK & DESSERTS RECIPES

Chocolate Torte

Servings: 12
Cooking Time: 35 Minutes

Ingredients:
- 5 eggs, separated, room temperature
- ¾ cup margarine, sliced
- What you'll need from store cupboard:
- 1 pkg. semisweet chocolate chips
- ½ cup Splenda
- ¼ tsp cream of tartar
- Nonstick cooking spray

Directions:
1. Heat oven to 350 degrees. Spray a 6-7-inch springform pan with cooking spray.
2. In a microwave safe bowl, melt chocolate chips and margarine, in 30 second intervals.
3. In a large bowl, beat egg yolks till thick and lemon colored. Beat in chocolate.
4. In a separate large bowl, with clean beaters, beat egg whites and cream of tartar till foamy. Beat in Splenda, 1 tablespoon at a time, till sugar is dissolved, continue beating till stiff glossy peaks form.
5. Fold ¼ of egg whites into chocolate mixture, then fold in the rest. Transfer to prepared pan. Bake 30-35 minutes, or center is set. Let cool completely before removing side of pan and serving.

Nutrition:
- InfoCalories 181 Total Carbs 10g Protein 3g Fat 14g Sugar 10g Fiber 0g

Caramel Pecan Pie

Servings:8
Cooking Time: 35 Minutes

Ingredients:

- 1 cup pecans, chopped
- ¾ cup almond milk, unsweetened
- 1/3 cup margarine, melted
- 1 tbsp. margarine, cold
- What you'll need from the store cupboard
- 2 cup almond flour
- ½ cup + 2 tablespoons Splenda for baking
- 1 tsp vanilla
- 1 tsp Arrowroot powder
- ¾ tsp sea salt
- ½ tsp vanilla
- ½ tsp maple syrup, sugar free
- Nonstick cooking spray

Directions:

1. Heat oven to 350 degrees. Spray a 9-inch pie pan with cooking spray.
2. In a medium bowl, combine flour, melted margarine, 2 tablespoons Splenda, and vanilla. Mix to thoroughly combine Ingredients. Press on bottom and sides of prepared pie pan. Bake 12 -15 minutes, or until edges start to brown. Set aside.
3. In a small sauce pan, combine milk, remaining Splenda, arrowroot, salt, ½ teaspoon vanilla, and syrup. Cook over medium heat until it starts to boil, stirring constantly. Keep cooking until it turns a gold color and starts to thicken, about 2-3 minutes. Remove from heat and let cool. Stir in ½ the pecans.
4. Pour the filling in the crust and top with remaining pecans. Bake about 15 minutes, or until filling starts to bubble. Cool completely before serving.

Nutrition:

- InfoCalories 375 Total Carbs 20g Net Carbs 15g Protein 7g Fat 30g Sugar 14g Fiber 5g

Peanut Butter Oatmeal Cookies

Servings: 20
Cooking Time: 30 Minutes

Ingredients:

- 2 egg whites
- ½ cup margarine, soft
- What you'll need from store cupboard:
- 1 cup flour
- 1 cup quick oats
- ½ cup reduced-fat peanut butter
- 1/3 cup Splenda
- 1/3 Splenda brown sugar
- ½ tsp baking soda
- ½ tsp vanilla

Directions:

1. Heat oven to 350 degrees.
2. In a large mixing bowl, combine dry Ingredients and stir to combine.
3. In a separate bowl, beat together the egg whites and margarine. Add to dry Ingredients and mix well.
4. Drop by teaspoonful onto nonstick cookie sheets. Bake 8-10 minutes or until edges start to brown.
5. Remove to wire rack and cool completely. Store in an airtight container. Serving size is 2 cookies.

Nutrition:

- InfoCalories 151 Total Carbs 17g Net Carbs 16g Protein 3g Fat 7g Sugar 7g Fiber 1g

Mini Eggplant Pizzas

Servings: 4
Cooking Time: 35 Minutes

Ingredients:
- 1 large eggplant, peeled and sliced into ¼ - inch circles
- 2 cup spaghetti sauce, (chapter 16)
- ½ cup reduced-fat mozzarella cheese, grated
- 2 eggs
- What you'll need from the store cupboard
- 1 ¼ cups Italian bread crumbs
- 1 tbsp. water
- ¼ tsp black pepper
- Nonstick cooking spray

Directions:
1. Heat oven to 350 degrees. Line 2 large cookie sheets with foil and spray well with cooking spray.
2. In a shallow dish, beat eggs, water and pepper. Place the bread crumbs in a separate shallow dish.
3. Dip eggplant pieces in egg mixture, then coat completely with bread crumbs. Place on prepared cookie sheets. Spray the tops with cooking spray and bake 15 minutes.
4. Turn the eggplant over and spray with cooking spray again. Bake another 15 minutes.
5. Remove from oven and top each piece with 1 tablespoon spaghetti sauce. Sprinkle cheese over sauce and bake another 4 – 5 minutes, or until sauce is bubbly and cheese is melted.

Nutrition:
- InfoCalories 171 Total Carbs 24g Net Carbs 20g Protein 9g Fat 5g Sugar 6g Fiber 4g

Raspberry & Dark Chocolate Mini Soufflés

Servings: 6

Cooking Time: 10 Minutes

Ingredients:

- 1 cup fresh raspberries
- 4 egg whites
- What you'll need from store cupboard:
- ½ oz. dark chocolate, chopped
- 6 tsp Splenda
- 1 tsp margarine, soft

Directions:

1. Heat oven to 400 degrees. Use the margarine to grease 6 small ramekins.
2. Puree the raspberries in a blender or food processor and press through a fine sieve to get all of the seeds out. Add 1 tablespoons Splenda and set aside.
3. Beat egg whites until thickened and start adding the remaining Splenda, gradually, until the mixture forms stiff glossy peaks.
4. Gently fold ⅓ of the egg whites into the raspberry puree. Once mixed, fold the raspberry puree mixture into the remaining egg whites and fold gently until there are no streaks of pink left.
5. Spoon the raspberry mixture into the ramekins filling them half full. Divide the chocolate between the ramekins and then fill to the top with soufflé mixture. Place ramekins on a baking sheet. Bake for 9 minutes until golden brown and puffed up. Serve immediately.

Nutrition:

- InfoCalories 60 Total Carbs 8g Net Carbs 7g Protein 3g Fat 1g Sugar 6g Fiber 1g

Gingerbread Cookies

Servings: 10
Cooking Time: 10 Minutes

Ingredients:

- 1 egg
- ¼ cup butter, soft
- What you'll need from store cupboard:
- 2 cup almond flour, sifted
- ¼ cup Splenda
- 1 tbsp. cinnamon
- 1 ½ tsp ginger
- 1 tsp vanilla
- ½ tsp baking powder
- ¼ tsp cloves
- ¼ tsp nutmeg

Directions:

1. In a medium bowl, stir together the almond flour, cinnamon, ginger, cloves, nutmeg, and baking powder.
2. In a large bowl, beat the butter and Splenda for 1-2 minutes, until fluffy. Beat in the egg and vanilla. Beat in the almond flour mixture until a dough forms.
3. Form the dough into a ball, wrap with plastic wrap and refrigerate for at least 30 minutes.
4. Heat the oven to 350 degrees. Line a cookie sheet with parchment paper.
5. Roll the dough out between two sheets of parchment paper to ¼-inch thick. Cut out desired shapes with cookie cutter and place on prepared pan. Or you can drop dough by teaspoonful onto pan.
6. Bake 10-15 minutes or until edges are golden brown. Remove to wire rack and cool. Store in airtight container. Serving size is 1 large, or 2 small cookies.

Nutrition:

- InfoCalories 181 Total Carbs 9g Net Carbs 7g Protein 5g Fat 15g Sugar 6g Fiber 2g

Coconut Milk Shakes

Servings: 2
Cooking Time: 5 Minutes

Ingredients:

- 1 ½ cup vanilla ice cream
- ½ cup coconut milk, unsweetened
- What you'll need from store cupboard:
- 2 ½ tbsp. coconut flakes
- 1 tsp unsweetened cocoa

Directions:

1. Heat oven to 350 degrees.
2. Place coconut on a baking sheet and bake, 2-3 minutes, stirring often, until coconut is toasted.
3. Place ice cream, milk, 2 tablespoons coconut, and cocoa in a blender and process until smooth.
4. Pour into glasses and garnish with remaining toasted coconut. Serve immediately.

Nutrition:

- InfoCalories 323 Total Carbs 23g Net Carbs 19g Protein 3g Fat 24g Sugar 18g Fiber 4g

Soft Pretzel Bites

Servings: 8
Cooking Time: 15 Minutes

Ingredients:

- 3 cups mozzarella cheese, grated
- 3 large eggs
- ½ cup cream cheese
- What you'll need from the store cupboard
- 2 cups almond flour, super fine
- 1 tbsp. baking powder
- 1 tbsp. coarse salt

Directions:

1. Heat oven to 400 degrees. Line a large cookie sheet with parchment paper.
2. Stir almond flour and baking powder together in a small bowl.
3. Place the mozzarella and cream cheese in a large glass bowl. Be sure to surround the cream cheese with the mozzarella. Melt the cheese in 30 second intervals on high, stirring after each interval. Continue this step until they are completely melted, about 2 – 2 ½ minutes.
4. Place the cheese, 2 eggs, and flour mixture into a food processor with a dough blade. Pulse on high until the mixture forms a uniform dough.
5. Wrap a pastry board with plastic wrap making sure it is taut. Lightly coat your hands with vegetable oil and separate dough into 8 equal parts. Roll each into 1-inch thick ropes.
6. With a sharp knife, cut dough into ¾-inch pieces. Place on prepared cookie sheet.
7. In a small bowl, whisk the remaining egg. Brush the dough pieces with egg then sprinkle with salt.
8. Bake 12 minutes, or until lightly browned. Set oven to broil and cook another 2 minutes to crisp up the outside of the pretzels. Serve warm by themselves or dip them in cheese sauce (chapter 16).

Nutrition:

- InfoCalories 242 Total Carbs 6g Net Carbs 3g Protein 11g Fat 20g Sugar 1g Fiber 3g

Chewy Granola Bars

Servings: 36

Cooking Time: 35 Minutes

Ingredients:

- 1 egg, beaten
- 2/3 cup margarine, melted
- What you'll need from store cupboard:
- 3 ½ cup quick oats
- 1 cup almonds, chopped
- ½ cup honey
- ½ cup sunflower kernels
- ½ cup coconut, unsweetened
- ½ cup dried apples
- ½ cup dried cranberries
- ½ cup Splenda brown sugar
- 1 tsp vanilla
- ½ tsp cinnamon
- Nonstick cooking spray

Directions:

1. Heat oven to 350 degrees. Spray a large baking sheet with cooking spray.
2. Spread oats and almonds on prepared pan. Bake 12-15 minutes until toasted, stirring every few minutes.
3. In a large bowl, combine egg, margarine, honey, and vanilla. Stir in remaining Ingredients.
4. Stir in oat mixture. Press into baking sheet and bake 13-18 minutes, or until edges are light brown.
5. Cool on a wire rack. Cut into bars and store in an airtight container.

Nutrition:

- InfoCalories 119 Total Carbs 13g Net Carbs 12g Protein 2g Fat 6g Sugar 7g Fiber 1g

Candied Pecans

Servings: 6
Cooking Time: 10 Minutes

Ingredients:

- 1 ½ tsp butter
- What you'll need from store cupboard:
- 1 ½ cup pecan halves
- 2 ½ tbsp. Splenda, divided
- 1 tsp cinnamon
- ¼ tsp ginger
- 1/8 tsp cardamom
- 1/8 tsp salt

Directions:

1. In a small bowl, stir together 1 1/2 teaspoons Splenda, cinnamon, ginger, cardamom and salt. Set aside.
2. Melt butter in a medium skillet over med-low heat. Add pecans, and two tablespoons Splenda. Reduce heat to low and cook, stirring occasionally, until sweetener melts, about 5 to 8 minutes.
3. Add spice mixture to the skillet and stir to coat pecans. Spread mixture to parchment paper and let cool for 10-15 minutes. Store in an airtight container. Serving size is ¼ cup.

Nutrition:

- InfoCalories 173 Total Carbs 8g Net Carbs 6g Protein 2g Fat 16g Sugar 6g Fiber 2g

Coconut Macaroni

Servings:5-6
Cooking Time: 15 Minutes

Ingredients:

- 100g of sweetened condensed milk
- 1 egg white
- 2 ml almond extract
- 2 ml vanilla extract
- A pinch of salt
- 175g unsweetened and shredded coconut

Directions:

1. Mix the condensed milk, egg white, almond extract, and salt in a bowl.
2. Add 160g of grated coconut and mix until well combined. The mixture must be able to maintain its shape.
3. Form 38 mm balls with your hands. In a separate dish, add 25 g of grated coconut.
4. Roll the coconut macaroni in the grated coconut until they are covered.
5. Preheat the air fryer for a few minutes and set the temperature to 150°C.
6. Add the coconut macaroni to the preheated air fryer. Set the time to 15 minutes at 150°C.
7. Let the macaroni cool for 5-10 minutes and serve when they finish cooling.

Nutrition:

- InfoCalories: 20 Fat: 0g Carbohydrates: 0g Protein: 0g Sugar: 0gCholesterol: 0mg

Popcorn Style Cauliflower

Servings: 4
Cooking Time: 20 Minutes

Ingredients:

- 1 head cauliflower, separated into bite-sized florets
- What you'll need from the store cupboard
- ¼ tsp garlic powder
- ¼ tsp salt
- 1/8 tsp black pepper
- Butter-flavored cooking spray

Directions:

1. Heat oven to 400 degrees.
2. Place cauliflower in a large bowl and spray with cooking spray, making sure to coat all sides. Sprinkle with seasonings and toss to coat.
3. Place in a single layer on a cookie sheet. Bake 20 – 25 minutes or until cauliflower starts to brown. Serve warm.

Nutrition:

- InfoCalories 53 Total Carbs 11g Net Carbs 6g Protein 4g Fat 0g Sugar 5g Fiber 5g

German Chocolate Cake Bars

Servings: 20

Cooking Time: 5 Minutes

Ingredients:

- 2 cup unsweetened coconut flakes
- 1 cup coconut milk, divided
- ¾ cup chopped pecans
- ¾ cup dark baking chocolate, chopped
- What you'll need from the store cupboard
- 1 ½ cup almond flour cracker crumbs (chapter 4)
- ½ cup + 2 tbsp. powdered sugar substitute
- ½ cup coconut oil
- Nonstick cooking spray

Directions:

1. Spray an 8x8-inch baking dish with cooking spray.
2. In a large bowl, combine the coconut, ½ cup sugar substitute, cracker crumbs and pecan, stir to combine.
3. In a medium sauce pan, combine ½ cup milk and oil, cook over medium heat until oil is melted and mixture is heated through. Pour over coconut mixture and stir to combine. Press evenly in prepared baking dish and chill 1-2 hours.
4. In a clean saucepan, place the chocolate and remaining milk over med-low heat. Cook, stirring constantly, until chocolate is melted and mixture is smooth. Add the 2 tablespoons sugar substitute and stir to combine.
5. Pour chocolate over the coconut layer and chill 1 hour, or until set. Cut into squares to serve.

Nutrition:

- InfoCalories 245 Total Carbs 12g Net Carbs 9g Protein 3g Fat 19g Sugar 7g Fiber 3g

OTHER FAVORITE RECIPES

Maple Shallot Vinaigrette

Servings: 4
Cooking Time: 5 Minutes

Ingredients:
- 1 tbsp. shallot, diced fine
- What you'll need from store cupboard:
- 2 tbsp. apple cider vinegar
- 1 tbsp. spicy brown mustard
- 1 tbsp. olive oil
- 2 tsp sugar free maple syrup

Directions:
1. Place all Ingredients in a small jar with an airtight lid. Shake well to mix. Refrigerate until ready to use. Serving size is 1 tablespoon.

Nutrition:
- InfoCalories 45 Total Carbs 5g Protein 0g Fat 2g Sugar 0g Fiber 0g

Crab & Cauliflower Bisque

Servings: 8
Cooking Time: 30 Minutes

Ingredients:

- 1 lb. lump crabmeat, cooked and shells removed
- 1 medium head cauliflower, separated into very small florets
- 1 white onion, diced fine
- 1 cup celery, diced fine
- 1 cup carrots, diced fine
- 1 cup half-n-half
- 1 tbsp. sherry
- 4 tbsp. margarine
- What you'll need from store cupboard:
- 6 cup chicken broth
- 1½ tsp coarse salt
- 1 tsp white pepper

Directions:

1. In a large saucepan, over med-high heat, melt margarine. Add celery, onion, and carrot. Cook, stirring frequently, until vegetables are tender.
2. Add in cauliflower, broth, salt, and pepper, and cook until soup starts to boil. Reduce heat to medium and cook 15 minutes, or until cauliflower is tender.
3. Pour into a blender and add cream and sherry. Process until combined and soup is smooth. Pour back into the saucepan.
4. Fold in crab and heat through. Serve.

Nutrition:

- InfoCalories 201 Total Carbs 10g Net Carbs 7g Protein 14g Fat 11g Sugar 4g Fiber 3g

Cheese Biscuits

Servings: 16
Cooking Time: 20 Minutes

Ingredients:

- 8 oz. low fat cream cheese
- 3 cup mozzarella cheese, grated
- 4 eggs
- 2 tbsp. margarine, melted
- What you'll need from store cupboard:
- 1-1/3 cup almond flour
- 4 tbsp. baking powder
- Nonstick cooking spray

Directions:

1. Heat oven to 400° degrees.   Spray a 12-inch cast iron skillet with cooking spray
2. In a saucepan over low heat, melt the cream cheese and mozzarella together. Stir until smooth. Remove from heat.
3. In a large bowl, combine the melted cheese, eggs, baking powder, and flour. Mix until smooth. Let rest for 10 to 20 minutes.
4. Use a large cookie scoop, to scoop dough and place in prepared skillet. Refrigerate 10 minutes.
5. Bake for 20 to 25 minutes, until golden brown. Brush biscuits with melted margarine.

Nutrition:

- InfoCalories 106 Total Carbs 5g Net Carbs 4g Protein 7g Fat 8g Sugar 0g Fiber 1g

Turkey Divan Casserole

Servings: 6
Cooking Time: 10 Minutes

Ingredients:
- Nonstick cooking spray
- 3 teaspoons extra-virgin olive oil, divided
- 1 pound turkey cutlets
- Pinch salt
- ¼ teaspoon freshly ground black pepper, divided
- ¼ cup chopped onion
- 2 garlic cloves, minced
- 2 tablespoons whole-wheat flour
- 1 cup unsweetened plain almond milk
- 1 cup low-sodium chicken broth
- ½ cup shredded Swiss cheese, divided
- ½ teaspoon dried thyme
- 4 cups chopped broccoli
- ¼ cup coarsely ground almonds

Directions:
1. Preheat the oven to 375°F. Spray a baking dish with nonstick cooking spray.
2. In a skillet, heat 1 teaspoon of oil over medium heat. Season the turkey with the salt and ⅛ teaspoon of pepper. Sauté the turkey cutlets for 5 to 7 minutes on each side until cooked through. Transfer to a cutting board, cool briefly, and cut into bite-size pieces.
3. In the same pan, heat the remaining 2 teaspoons of oil over medium-high heat. Sauté the onion for 3 minutes until it begins to soften. Add the garlic and continue cooking for another minute.
4. Stir in the flour and mix well. Whisk in the almond milk, broth, and remaining ⅛ teaspoon of pepper, and continue whisking until smooth. Add ¼ cup of cheese and the thyme, and continue stirring until the cheese is melted.
5. In the prepared baking dish, arrange the broccoli on the bottom. Cover with half the sauce. Place the turkey pieces on top of the broccoli, and cover with the remaining sauce. Sprinkle with the remaining ¼ cup of cheese and the ground almonds.
6. Bake for 35 minutes until the sauce is bubbly and the top is browned.

Nutrition:
- Info Calories: 207; Total Fat: 8g; Protein: 25g; Carbohydrates: 9g; Sugars: 2g; Fiber: 3g; Sodium: 128mg

Turkey Chili

Servings: 6
Cooking Time: 15 Minutes

Ingredients:

- 1 tablespoon extra-virgin olive oil
- 1 pound lean ground turkey
- 1 large onion, diced
- 3 garlic cloves, minced
- 1 red bell pepper, seeded and diced
- 1 cup chopped celery
- 2 tablespoons chili powder
- 1 tablespoon ground cumin
- 1 (28-ounce) can reduced-salt diced tomatoes
- 1 (15-ounce) can low-sodium kidney beans, drained and rinsed
- 2 cups low-sodium chicken broth
- ½ teaspoon salt
- Shredded cheddar cheese, for serving (optional)

Directions:

1. In a large pot, heat the oil over medium heat. Add the turkey, onion, and garlic, and cook, stirring regularly, until the turkey is cooked through.
2. Add the bell pepper, celery, chili powder, and cumin. Stir well and continue to cook for 1 minute.
3. Add the tomatoes with their liquid, kidney beans, and chicken broth. Bring to a boil, reduce the heat to low, and simmer for 20 minutes.
4. Season with the salt and serve topped with cheese (if using).

Nutrition:

- Info Calories: 276; Total Fat: 10g; Protein: 23g; Carbohydrates: 27g; Sugars: 7g; Fiber: 8g; Sodium: 556mg

Homemade Turkey Breakfast Sausage

Servings: 8 (1 Patty Each)
Cooking Time: 10 Minutes

Ingredients:

- 1 pound lean ground turkey
- ½ teaspoon salt
- ½ teaspoon dried sage
- ½ teaspoon dried thyme
- ½ teaspoon freshly ground black pepper
- ¼ teaspoon ground fennel seeds
- 1 teaspoon extra-virgin olive oil

Directions:

1. In a large mixing bowl, combine the ground turkey, salt, sage, thyme, pepper, and fennel. Mix well.
2. Shape the meat into 8 small, round patties.
3. Heat the olive oil in a skillet over medium-high heat. Cook the patties in the skillet for 3 to 4 minutes on each side until browned and cooked through.
4. Serve warm, or store in an airtight container in the refrigerator for up to 3 days or in the freezer for up to 1 month.

Nutrition:

- Info Calories: 92; Total Fat: 5g; Protein: 11g; Carbohydrates: 0g; Sugars: 0g; Fiber: 0g; Sodium: 156mg

Red Pepper, Goat Cheese, And Arugula Open-faced Grilled Sandwich

Servings: 1

Cooking Time: 5 Minutes

Ingredients:
- ½ red bell pepper, seeded
- Nonstick cooking spray
- 1 slice whole-wheat thin-sliced bread (I love Ezekiel sprouted bread and Dave's Killer Bread)
- 2 tablespoons crumbled goat cheese
- Pinch dried thyme
- ½ cup arugula

Directions:
1. Preheat the broiler to high. Line a baking sheet with parchment paper.
2. Cut the ½ bell pepper lengthwise into two pieces and arrange on the prepared baking sheet with the skin facing up.
3. Broil for 5 to 10 minutes until the skin is blackened. Transfer to a covered container to steam for 5 minutes, then remove the skin from the pepper using your fingers. Cut the pepper into strips.
4. Heat a small skillet over medium-high heat. Spray it with nonstick cooking spray and place the bread in the skillet. Top with the goat cheese and sprinkle with the thyme. Pile the arugula on top, followed by the roasted red pepper strips. Press down with a spatula to hold in place.
5. Cook for 2 to 3 minutes until the bread is crisp and browned and the cheese is warmed through. (If you prefer, you can make a half-closed sandwich instead: Cut the bread in half and place one half in the skillet. Top with the cheese, thyme, arugula, red pepper, and the other half slice of bread. Cook for 4 to 6 minutes, flipping once, until both sides are browned.)

Nutrition:
- Info Calories: 109; Total Fat: 2g; Protein: 4g; Carbohydrates: 21g; Sugars: 5g; Fiber: 6g; Sodium: 123mg

Clam & Bacon Soup

Servings: 8
Cooking Time: 20 Minutes

Ingredients:

- 10-12 large clams, in the shell
- 4 slices bacon, chopped and cooked almost crisp
- 3 cups cauliflower, separated into florets
- ½ cup onion, diced
- What you'll need from store cupboard:
- 6 cup water
- 1 tsp Worcestershire sauce

Directions:

1. Scrub clams and rinse under cold running water. Place in a large pot and add water. Bring to a simmer over med-high heat. Cover and cook until clams open, about 8-10 minutes. Transfer clams to bowl to cool.
2. Cook onion in the same pan used for the bacon, 2-3 minutes. Stir to scrape up the brown bits on the bottom of the pan.
3. When clams are cool enough to touch, remove the meat from the shells and chop it.
4. Bring the clam liquid to a boil. Add cauliflower and cook until almost tender, about 5 minutes.
5. Stir in the bacon, Worcestershire sauce and clams. Season with salt and pepper to taste and cook until everything is heated through. Serve immediately.

Nutrition:

- InfoCalories 105 Total Carbs 4g Protein 7g Fat 7g Sugar 2g Fiber 1g

Cabbage Slaw Salad

Servings: 6
Cooking Time: 15 Minutes

Ingredients:

- 2 cups finely chopped green cabbage
- 2 cups finely chopped red cabbage
- 2 cups grated carrots
- 3 scallions, both white and green parts, sliced
- 2 tablespoons extra-virgin olive oil
- 2 tablespoons rice vinegar
- 1 teaspoon honey
- 1 garlic clove, minced
- ¼ teaspoon salt

Directions:

1. In a large bowl, toss together the green and red cabbage, carrots, and scallions.
2. In a small bowl, whisk together the oil, vinegar, honey, garlic, and salt.
3. Pour the dressing over the veggies and mix to thoroughly combine.
4. Serve immediately, or cover and chill for several hours before serving.

Nutrition:

- Info Calories: 80; Total Fat: 5g; Protein: 1g; Carbohydrates: 10g; Sugars: 6g; Fiber: 3g; Sodium: 126mg

Sprig Of Parsley

Servings: 3
Cooking Time:2 Minutes

Ingredients:

- Fresh parsley -1/4 cup
- Watercress – ½ cup
- Frozen strawberries – ½ cup
- Frozen banana – ½
- Chia seeds – 1 tsp.
- Plant-based protein powder – 1 scoop
- Water to blend

Directions:

1. Blend everything in a blender.
2. Serve.

Nutrition:

- Info 214 Fat: 4Carb: 46g Protein: 29g

Herb Vinaigrette

Servings: 12
Cooking Time: 5 Minutes

Ingredients:
- 2 tbsp. shallot, diced fine
- 1 tbsp. fresh basil, diced
- 1 tbsp. fresh oregano, diced
- 1 tbsp. fresh tarragon, diced
- What you'll need from store cupboard:
- ¼ cup extra virgin olive oil
- ¼ cup low sodium chicken broth
- ¼ cup red-wine vinegar
- ¼ teaspoon salt
- ¼ teaspoon freshly ground pepper

Directions:
1. Place all Ingredients in a jar with an air tight lid. Secure lid and shake vigorously to combine.
2. Refrigerate until ready to use. Will keep up to 2 days. Serving size is 1 tablespoon.

Nutrition:
- InfoCalories 39 Total Carbs 0 Protein 0g Fat 4g Sugar 0g Fiber 0g

Scallops And Asparagus Skillet

Servings: 4

Cooking Time: 10 Minutes

Ingredients:

- 3 teaspoons extra-virgin olive oil, divided
- 1 pound asparagus, trimmed and cut into 2-inch segments
- 1 tablespoon butter
- 1 pound sea scallops
- ¼ cup dry white wine
- Juice of 1 lemon
- 2 garlic cloves, minced
- ¼ teaspoon freshly ground black pepper

Directions:

1. In a large skillet, heat 1½ teaspoons of oil over medium heat.
2. Add the asparagus and sauté for 5 to 6 minutes until just tender, stirring regularly. Remove from the skillet and cover with aluminum foil to keep warm.
3. Add the remaining 1½ teaspoons of oil and the butter to the skillet. When the butter is melted and sizzling, place the scallops in a single layer in the skillet. Cook for about 3 minutes on one side until nicely browned. Use tongs to gently loosen and flip the scallops, and cook on the other side for another 3 minutes until browned and cooked through. Remove and cover with foil to keep warm.
4. In the same skillet, combine the wine, lemon juice, garlic, and pepper. Bring to a simmer for 1 to 2 minutes, stirring to mix in any browned pieces left in the pan.
5. Return the asparagus and the cooked scallops to the skillet to coat with the sauce. Serve warm.

Nutrition:

- Info Calories: 252; Total Fat: 7g; Protein: 26g; Carbohydrates: 15g; Sugars: 3g; Fiber: 2g; Sodium: 493mg

Falafel With Creamy Garlic-yogurt Sauce

Servings: 4

Cooking Time: 15 Minutes

Ingredients:

- FOR THE SAUCE
- ¾ cup plain nonfat Greek yogurt
- 3 garlic cloves, minced
- Juice of 1 lemon
- 1 tablespoon extra-virgin olive oil
- ¼ teaspoon salt
- FOR THE FALAFEL
- 1 (15-ounce) can low-sodium chickpeas, drained and rinsed
- 2 garlic cloves, roughly chopped
- 2 tablespoons whole-wheat flour
- 2 tablespoons chopped fresh parsley
- ½ teaspoon ground cumin
- ¼ teaspoon salt
- 2 teaspoons canola oil, divided
- 8 large lettuce leaves, chopped
- 1 cucumber, chopped
- 1 tomato, diced

Directions:

1. TO MAKE THE SAUCE
2. In a small bowl, combine the yogurt, garlic, lemon juice, olive oil, and salt, and mix well. Cover and refrigerate until ready to serve.
3. TO MAKE THE FALAFEL
4. In a food processor or blender, combine the chickpeas and garlic, and pulse until chopped well but not creamy. Add the flour, parsley, cumin, and salt. Pulse several more times until incorporated.
5. Using your hands, form the mixture into balls, using about 1 tablespoon of mixture for each ball.
6. In a medium skillet, heat 1 teaspoon of canola oil over medium-high heat. Working in batches, add the falafel to the skillet, cooking on each side for 2 to 3 minutes until browned and crisp. Remove the falafel from the skillet, and repeat with the remaining oil and falafel until all are cooked.
7. Divide the lettuce, cucumber, and tomato among 4 plates.
8. Top each plate with 2 falafel and 2 tablespoons of sauce. Serve immediately.

Nutrition:

- Info Calories: 219; Total Fat: 8g; Protein: 12g; Carbohydrates: 27g; Sugars: 6g; Fiber: 7g; Sodium: 462mg

RECIPES INDEX

Printed in Great Britain
by Amazon

Who Is Sherlock?

Essays on Identity in Modern Holmes Adaptations

Edited by LYNNETTE PORTER

McFarland & Company, Inc., Publishers

Jefferson, North Carolina

ISBN (print) 978-0-7864-9907-6
ISBN (ebook) 0-1-4766-2651-3

LIBRARY OF CONGRESS CATALOGUING DATA ARE AVAILABLE

BRITISH LIBRARY CATALOGUING DATA ARE AVAILABLE

Front cover image of Benedict Cumberbatch as Sherlock Holmes
in *Sherlock*, 2016 (PBS/Photofest)

Printed in the United States of America

*McFarland & Company, Inc., Publishers
Box 611, Jefferson, North Carolina 28640
www.mcfarlandpub.com*

Who Is Sherlock?

ALSO BY LYNNETTE PORTER
AND FROM MCFARLAND

Van Gogh in Popular Culture (2016)

The Doctor Who *Franchise: American Influence,
Fan Culture and the Spinoffs* (2012)

*Tarnished Heroes, Charming Villains and Modern
Monsters: Science Fiction in Shades of Gray
on 21st Century Television* (2010)

EDITED BY LYNNETTE PORTER

*Sherlock Holmes for the 21st Century:
Essays on New Adaptations* (2012)